AF892586

Controversies in Criminology and Criminal Justice

NORBERT EBISIKE

SUNBURY PRESS
Mechanicsburg, Pennsylvania USA

Published by Sunbury Press, Inc.
50 West Main Street, Suite A
Mechanicsburg, Pennsylvania 17055

www.sunburypress.com

Copyright © 2014 by Norbert Ebisike.
Cover copyright © 2013 by Sunbury Press, Inc.

Sunbury Press supports copyright. Copyright fuels creativity, encourages diverse voices, promotes free speech, and creates a vibrant culture. Thank you for buying an authorized edition of this book and for complying with copyright laws by not reproducing, scanning, or distributing any part of it in any form without permission. You are supporting writers and allowing Sunbury Press to continue to publish books for every reader. For information contact Sunbury Press, Inc., Subsidiary Rights Dept., 50-A W. Main St., Mechanicsburg, PA 17011 USA or legal@sunburypress.com.

For information about special discounts for bulk purchases, please contact Sunbury Press Orders Dept. at (855) 338-8359 or orders@sunburypress.com.

To request one of our authors for speaking engagements or book signings, please contact Sunbury Press Publicity Dept. at publicity@sunburypress.com.

ISBN: 978-1-62006-321-7 (Trade Paperback)
ISBN: 978-1-62006-322-4 (Mobipocket)
ISBN: 978-1-62006-323-1 (ePub)

FIRST SUNBURY PRESS EDITION: December 2013

Product of the United States of America
0 1 1 2 3 5 8 13 21 34 55

Set in Bookman Old Style
Designed by Lawrence Knorr
Cover by Lawrence Knorr
Edited by Janice Rhayem

Continue the Enlightenment!

CONTENTS

PREFACE

This book examines some of the most contentious issues in criminology and criminal justice. The issues examined are plea bargaining, the use of psychics in crime investigations, personalizing firearms, the e-mail scams, and terrorism. No single day passes without news reports on terrorism, firearm-related deaths, internet crimes, unsolved murders, as well as plea negotiations. These issues always make millions of people ask the question of what is to be done; these issues always provoke feelings of anger and utter despair. In this highly provocative book, the question of what is to be done has been addressed.

This book is made up of five chapters. Chapter one examines the issue of plea bargaining. Plea bargaining is a process whereby an agreement is made between the prosecutor and the defendant, in which the defendant agrees to plead guilty or no contest, and the prosecutor, in return, agrees to dismiss some of the charges, reduce a charge to a lesser charge, or recommend to the judge to give a particular sentence. In some cases the prosecutor may dismiss all the charges against a defendant, and in return the defendant will testify against codefendants. The controversy surrounding plea bargaining stems from the fact that more than 95 percent of criminal cases are disposed through guilty pleas, without a trial. This book argues that plea bargaining does not provide adequate protection and safeguards for the innocent defendant. There are also ethical issues surrounding plea bargaining. For instance, where accused persons maintain their innocence, is it unethical for the defense counsel to insist that they plead guilty? Plea bargaining is in the best interests of a guilty defendant. The guilty should be adequately punished, not given discounts. The offender needs rehabilitation, not rebates. Plea bargaining can also be seen as a form of trade discounts, whereby you "buy one and get one free" or you buy one and get the other one for half price. Under plea bargaining, prosecutors and defense attorneys do not develop trial skills. This results in the skills of good advocacy being lost. The criminal justice system becomes weak because we do not have skilled advocates. Plea bargaining also re-victimizes. This book maintains that the disadvantages of plea bargaining far outweigh the advantages and calls on the United States Supreme Court to re-visit the issue. Plea bargaining should be abolished.

Should psychics be used in crime investigations? Is there a scientific basis to psychic abilities? Should psychics be allowed to testify in courts? These questions and many more have been addressed in chapter two. At the moment there is no general agreement in the scientific community on the scientific basis of psychic abilities. However, it is commonly acknowledged that there are certain phenomena that cannot be explained under the normal senses and circumstances. Currently, there are problems with proving psychic abilities. However, and as some scholars have pointed out, "nonproof does not constitute disproof." Similarly, Arthur Lyons and Marcello Truzzi have noted the fact that there are certain phenomena that cannot be explained scientifically at the moment, but that does not mean that they are not scientifically explainable. It is submitted that there is some truth about psychic abilities. Are there neurobiological explanations of psi abilities? Some studies have shown that there is a relationship between brain waves and the mental states associated with psi abilities. A positive relationship between alpha brain waves and clairvoyance and telepathy has been shown by some studies. Is precognition a normal brain function? There is evidence to suggest that precognition may actually be a normal brain function that involves brain voltage. Psychics can assist in crime investigations in many ways, and these have been discussed. Psychics have assisted the police in crime investigations in many cases, especially in the United States. Examples of such cases have been outlined in this book. Expert testimony by psychics is generally inadmissible. However, in a murder case in

California in 2006, a psychic was allowed to testify in court. The judge got it wrong in this case, as the psychic should not have been allowed to testify. This case has been critically examined. Fundamentally, this book argues that psychics should be used in crime investigations. However, psychics should not be allowed to testify in court, because their method lacks adequate foundation as to be introduced into the courtroom as evidence at the moment.

Chapter three examines the issue of personalizing firearms. Improvements in the safety mechanisms or measures of certain products usually reduce injuries from such products. Hence, many scholars have called for the application of such safety measures to firearms. One of such safety measures is to personalize firearms. Personalizing firearms involves designing firearms with personalized identification technology so that only the authorized user(s) can fire the gun. The idea of personalizing guns is not new, but it still has not been adopted by some of the firearm manufacturers. Furthermore, there are still no federal laws mandating the use of such devices in the design of firearms manufactured in the United States. This chapter therefore, examines the reasons for this neglect and argues that biometrics has a very important role to play in our efforts to prevent and reduce firearm-related injuries and deaths. The various ways of personalizing firearms include fitting firearms with electronic locks, designing firearms with fingerprint sensors, equipping firearms with radio frequency identification device, operating firearms with a remote control, and designing firearms with a touch memory pad. After a critical examination of these methods of personalizing firearms, it is submitted that equipping the trigger of firearms with sensors that can identify the authorized user through fingerprint is the best option. Personalizing firearms will lead to higher costs of firearms, but taking a costs-benefits approach, this book argues that the benefits of personalizing firearms far outweigh the costs.

In chapter four, the Nigerian 419 e-mail scam has been discussed. Billions of dollars have been scammed out of many people throughout the world, yet the scam continues. In this chapter, the following questions have been addressed: why Nigerians? Who falls for these scams? Are some victims to be blamed? What is to be done to stop the scam? In order to answer these questions there has been a critical examination of some of the 419 scam letters, as well as an examination of the social-economic background of some of the victims. One of the main arguments of this chapter is that in almost all the 419 scam letters the criminal intent is obvious. Therefore, victims of such cases where the criminal intent is obvious should be prosecuted. Is there a typical profile of individuals who are likely to become victims? There is no typical profile of potential victims, per se. However, one of the key factors in becoming a 419 scam victim is greed. Based on the socio-economic background of majority of the victims examined for this book, the advance fee scam specifically appears to be a middle class and upper class phenomenon. This claim merits further research, however. This chapter also discusses the largest officially recorded 419 scam loss, which is the $242 million scam involving three Nigerians. They were convicted of scamming the head of International Finance at a Brazilian bank. The bank collapsed as a result of this scam. As has been suggested by some scholars, Internet Service Providers should be held more accountable for the misuse of e-mail accounts. The idea of using digital identity cards is necessary and hereby supported. This book concludes that most of the victims are to be blamed and calls for the prosecution of some of these victims. There were warning signs throughout the process, but because of greed they fell into the trap. These warning signs have been clearly outlined in this book.

Chapter five discusses the issue of terrorism. Terrorist attacks are like earthquakes. We do not know when they will happen, but what we do know is that they are likely to happen. Therefore, we have to prepare for them. What are the causes of terrorism? The psychological, biological, and environmental explanations of terrorism have been examined. This chapter presents an easy to understand examination of the strategies for combating terrorism and for stopping and containing the fundamentalist ideologies that are fueling and supporting terrorism. The current United States national strategy for combating terrorism has been critically discussed. Is there a link between past criminality and terrorist potential? An examination of the background of some terrorist operatives reveals a link between past history of crime and involvement in terrorist acts. This link, however, does not exist with the leaders of the terrorist groups. There are many ways through which terrorist groups end, and these have been critically examined. Al-Qaeda seeks unobtainable goals and will eventually disintegrate.

In this book, the author addresses these controversial and sensitive issues in an easy to understand manner without any restraint. The general public, students, and policy makers who want answers to all the questions raised in this book will find this book an eye-opener.

Norbert Ebisike, SJD
Philadelphia, Pennsylvania

CHAPTER 1
UNDERSTANDING PLEA BARGAINING

1.1 INTRODUCTION

> The Supreme Court unleashed a runaway train when it sanctioned plea bargaining in *Bordenkircher v. Hayes*. Despite a steady media diet of titillating criminal trials in recent years, there is an increasing recognition that jury trials are now a rarity in America, and that something, somewhere is amiss. That "something" is plea bargaining.[1]

Plea bargaining is one of the most controversial issues in criminal justice. There are several reasons for this controversy. First, is the fact that in the United States the percentage of criminal cases disposed through guilty pleas is in the high 90s. Recent data from the Department of Justice, Bureau of Justice Statistics indicate that in the United States 97 percent of federal convictions and 94 percent of state convictions are the result of guilty pleas. Thus, many scholars have argued that plea bargaining is unconstitutional and should be abolished. Second, it has been recognized that plea bargaining forces innocent defendants to plead guilty to crimes that they did not commit. Above all, under plea bargaining, a defendant gives up some of his constitutional rights, such as: (a) The right to trial by jury, (b) the right to call witnesses, as well as the right to cross-examine adverse witnesses, (c) the right to a public hearing, and (d) the right to not be convicted without proof beyond a reasonable doubt.

This chapter provides a critical analysis of plea bargaining and argues that plea bargaining does not uphold one of the main reasons for establishing a judicial system, which is to ensure that justice is served. Plea bargaining does not provide adequate protection and safeguards for the innocent defendant. The Supreme Court's indifference makes one believe that plea bargaining is simply a vehicle to reduce caseloads, rather than a vehicle for justice. Similarly, this book raises the issue of whether plea bargaining is just another instrument used by the government to reduce overcrowding in prisons. Defendants pleading guilty receive lesser sentences and consequently this leads to lesser prison congestion. Plea bargaining raises some ethical issues. Where an accused person maintains her innocence, is it unethical for the defense counsel to insist that she pleads guilty? There is no gainsaying the fact that plea bargaining assists the criminal justice system. However, in the long run, the disadvantages of plea bargaining far outweigh its advantages. Trial by a judge is an alternative to plea bargaining. Plea bargaining is in the best interest of a guilty defendant.

1.2 WHAT IS PLEA BARGAINING?

Plea bargaining is a practice whereby a defendant agrees to forgo a trial and instead decides to plead guilty or no contest to the charges being brought against him or her. As part of the plea agreement, the prosecutor may decide to dismiss some of the charges or reduce a charge to a lesser charge. The prosecutor may also make a recommendation to the judge to give the defendant a particular sentence. In some cases, the prosecutor may dismiss all the charges against a defendant, and in return, the defendant will testify against codefendants. Plea bargaining can also be defined as "any process in which inducements are offered in exchange for a defendant's cooperation in not fully contesting the charges against him."[2] It is "a nontrial procedure for convicting and condemning people accused of serious crimes."[3] Plea bargaining is nothing but a system of condemnation without adjudication.[4] As John Langbein has pointed out, "it is a system that replaces trial, which is what our constitution intends, with deals. Second, those deals are coerced. The prosecutor is basically forcing people to waive their rights to jury trial by threatening them with ever greater sanctions if they refuse to plead and instead demand the right to jury trial."[5] Plea bargaining operates by threats and promises. Plea bargaining is also known as negotiated plea or plea agreement. Every plea bargain must be approved by a judge.

Plea bargaining is a form of contract, and it can be revoked by either party before the plea is approved by the court. Therefore, conditions are attached, such as the defendant agreeing to reveal the names of others involved in the crime, agreeing to admit involvement in other crimes, testifying against a co-defendant, and so on. The main condition, however, is that the defendant agrees to plead guilty. Plea bargains, being contracts, must be fulfilled. This was confirmed in *Santobello v. New York*,[6] where the United States Supreme Court stated that "when a plea rests in any significant degree on a promise or agreement of the prosecutor, so that it can be said to be part of the inducement or consideration, such promise must be fulfilled."[7]

In *Santobello v. New York,* the defendant was indicted on two felony counts of promoting gambling in the first degree and possession of gambling records in the first degree.[8] The defendant entered into a plea negotiation with the assistant district attorney, in which the defendant agreed to plead guilty to a lesser offense of possession of gambling records in the second degree. As part of the plea agreement, the assistant district attorney agreed not to make any recommendation to the court regarding the sentence. The court accepted the plea negotiation and set a date for the sentencing. The sentencing date was postponed, and before a new date was scheduled, the defendant hired a new attorney and filed a motion to withdraw the guilty plea. The motion was denied by the court. A new prosecutor took over the case and recommended that the defendant be given the maximum sentence of one year imprisonment. The defendant objected. It was reported that the new prosecutor was not aware of the earlier plea agreement where the first prosecutor agreed not to make any recommendation with regards to the sentence. The judge imposed the maximum sentence, and stated that he was not influenced by the prosecutor's recommendation, but rather based the sentence on the presentence report.

The defendant appealed. The appellate division of the Supreme Court of New York affirmed the conviction and denied the defendant leave to appeal to the New York Court of Appeals.[9] The case went to the United States Supreme Court, which granted certiorari. The United States Supreme Court, through Chief Justice Burger, held that:

> In expressing the unanimous view of the court, that the disposition of criminal charges by agreement between the prosecutor and the accused—which was an essential component of the administration of justice, to be encouraged when properly administered—must be attended by safeguards, that when a guilty plea rested in significant degree on a promise of the prosecutor, so that it could be said to be part of the inducement, such promise must be fulfilled, and that the state court's affirmance of the conviction was improper in the case at bar, it being immaterial that the breach of agreement by the prosecution was inadvertent.[10]

Concurring, Justice Douglas stated that where the prosecutor did not fulfill the plea agreement, the case must be vacated and in such cases, the state has to decide based on the circumstances of each case "whether due process required that there be specific performance of the plea bargain, or that the defendant be given the option to go to trial on the original charges, the defendant's preference to be given considerable, if not controlling weight in choosing the appropriate remedy."[11] Chief Justice Burger also said,

> We need not reach the question whether the sentencing judge would or would not have been influenced had he known all the details of the

> negotiations for the plea. He stated that the prosecutor's recommendation did not influence him and we have no reason to doubt that. Nevertheless, we conclude that the interests of justice and appropriate recognition of the duties of the prosecution in relation to promises made in the negotiation of pleas of guilty will be best served by remanding the case to the state courts for further consideration. The ultimate relief to which petitioner is entitled we leave to the discretion of the state court, which is in a better position to decide whether the circumstances of this case require only that there be specific performance of the agreement on the plea, in which case petitioner should be resentenced by a different judge, or whether, in the view of the state court, the circumstances require granting the relief sought by petitioner, *i.e.,* the opportunity to withdraw his plea of guilty. We emphasize that this is in sense to question the fairness of the sentencing judge; the fault here rests on the prosecutor, not on the sentencing judge.[12]

The United States Supreme Court therefore vacated the judgment of the appellate court and remanded the case for reconsideration. The Supreme Court went on to state that "the staff lawyers in a prosecutor's office have the burden of letting the left hand know what the right hand is doing or has done. That a breach of agreement is inadvertent does not lessen its impact."[13] Prosecutorial procedures must be followed accordingly. The issue of heavy workload that may exist in a prosecutor's office is not an acceptable excuse for ignoring prosecutorial procedures.[14] The Supreme Court was right in this decision. As we have seen, once the court accepts a plea bargain, it must be fulfilled. Having said that, plea bargains are ridiculous. Plea bargaining can also be seen as a form of trade discounts, whereby you "buy one and get one free," or you buy one and get the other one for half price. Thus, plea bargaining is an incentive offered by a prosecutor to a defendant so that the defendant can plead guilty to the charges being brought against him.

There are two main types of plea bargaining: charge bargaining and sentence bargaining. Charge bargaining is a type of plea bargaining whereby the defendant pleads guilty or no contest, and the prosecutor, in exchange, drops some of the charges or reduces the charge to a less serious charge. For instance, a prosecutor may offer a defendant charged with burglary, the chance to plead guilty to a lesser charge of attempted burglary. Sentence bargaining, on the other hand, refers to the type of plea bargaining whereby the defendant agrees to plead guilty or no contest, and the prosecutor offers to recommend a lighter sentence for the charges.

1.3 KEY ELEMENTS OF PLEA BARGAINING

There are certain constitutional requirements or safeguards that have to be met before a plea bargain can be valid. The rationale behind this requirement is that because a defendant is waiving some of his important rights and privileges, it becomes plausible and crucial to ensure that these rights and privileges are being waived voluntarily.

Plea Bargaining Procedure

Every plea bargaining negotiation must follow certain procedures. The Federal Rules of Criminal Procedure[15] provide that:

(a) The prosecutor and the defendant's attorney, or the defendant, if he or she represents himself or herself, can reach a plea agreement.
(b) The court is not allowed to be a party to the discussions and terms.
(c) After the plea agreement has been met, the court may accept or reject the agreement, or even defer a decision until the court has reviewed the defendant's presentence report.

(d) The plea agreement must be disclosed in open court, unless for a good cause, it can be disclosed on camera.

Under Rule 11 of the Federal Rules of Criminal Procedure, judges are not allowed to take part in plea negotiations.[16] The reasons for this have been clearly outlined by Sarah Welling as follows:

> The risk of coercion arises if the trial judge proposes a plea bargain which the defendant rejects. Trial judges like guilty pleas because guilty pleas minimize their workload and eliminate the risk of reversal on appeal. Thus a defendant who rejects a plea bargain offer endorsed by the judge and demands a trial may irritate the judge. The defendant then goes to trial, usually before the judge whose offer he has refused, and the defendant may risk a slanted trial or a disproportionally heavy sentence if convicted. Thus, judicial participation in plea bargaining puts some pressure on the defendant to plead guilty. Judicial participation also creates an appearance of impropriety since it brings the judge down to the level of a negotiating litigant.[17]

However, some scholars believe that judicial participation in plea negotiations may assist in ensuring that defendants enter into intelligent pleas, and also may ensure better sentencing since the judge will have more information about the case as he was involved in the plea negotiations.[18] The fact remains, however, that under the Federal Rules of Criminal Procedure 11, courts are not permitted to take part in plea discussions. It should be noted, that "because the federal prohibition on judicial participation in plea negotiations is not constitutional, states are free to permit participation. Although some states agree with the federal approach prohibiting participation, many states allow judges to participate in plea discussions."[19]

In *United States v. Adams*[20] the district court judge participated in the plea negotiations. On appeal, the United States Court of Appeals for the 5th Circuit restated the provision of Fed. R. Crim. P. 11, which prohibits courts from participating in plea negotiations. Delivering the opinion of the Court of Appeals, Justice Randall stated that:

> Although the details of the trial judge's participation in the negotiations leading to Adams' plea are unclear, the record leaves no doubt that there was a substantial violation of this prohibition. Unfortunately, Adams does not raise this issue on appeal; the two-page argument in his brief does not even mention Rule 11. The record discloses, however, that the trial judge participated in plea discussions on at least two occasions. First, she discussed the bargain with Garner and Ethington before the two had reached an agreement, in a meeting in her chambers on August 29; although the precise nature of her comments are unclear, the record shows that she at least approved (if only tentatively) an arrangement whereby Adams would plead guilty and would be placed on probation. Second, sometime before Adams' second arraignment, on November 21, 1979, the judge offered a plea bargain to Adams on her own initiative, i.e., that he plead guilty to two counts in exchange for four years' imprisonment on one and four years' probation on the other.[21]

Justice Randall stated that the district judge's participation in the plea discussions was plain error sufficient for the Court of Appeals to raise the issue sua sponte, pursuant to Fed.R.Crim.P. 52(b). Justice Randall cited the decision in *United States v. Werker,* where it was held that "as a result of his participation, the judge is no longer a judicial officer or a neutral arbiter. Rather, he becomes or seems to become an advocate for the resolution he has suggested to the defendant." Justice Randall also said:

> To sum up; in the absence of a showing of actual prejudice, a new trial is unnecessary as part of the protective scheme prescribed by Rule 11(e), but would entail serious costs in judicial resources. On the other hand, a new sentencing hearing would provide an important measure of protection against judicial participation in plea discussions, and entail little costs in judicial resources. Taken together, these factors lead us to the conclusion that a defendant who has pled not guilty after an unsuccessful plea discussion, in which the judge has participated, but who makes no showing of actual prejudice as a result of the judge's participation, should not receive a new trial but should be resentenced before a different judge. We intimate no belief as to the actual impartiality of the district court judge who heard this case, or as to the propriety of the sentence she rendered. Our remand for resentencing before a different judge is intended instead, to extend the prophylactic scheme established by Rule 11 in order to protect defendants from the potential (but difficult to prove) effects of judicial participation in plea negotiations, and to prevent to the greatest practical extent the misimpression created by such participation.[22]

In a nutshell, the Court of Appeals affirmed the judgment in part and reversed in part. The case was remanded for resentencing by a different judge.

Constitutional Rights

Fundamentally, a defendant who agrees to enter a plea bargaining agreement, in effect relinquishes some of his constitutional rights and privileges, including:

(a) The Fifth Amendment privilege against self-incrimination.

(b) The Sixth Amendment right to speedy and public trial by jury.
(c) The due process right to be acquitted unless found guilty beyond a reasonable doubt.
(d) The right to call witnesses and to confront adverse witnesses.

It must be made clear to the defendant that he is waiving these constitutional rights before the plea agreement can be accepted. This requirement was confirmed in *Boykin v. Alabama,*[23] as well as in *McCarthy v. United States.*[24] In *Boykin v. Alabama,*

> Petitioner, a 27 year-old African American, who was represented by appointed counsel, pleaded guilty to five indictments for common-law robbery. The judge asked no questions of petitioner concerning his plea, and petitioner did not address the court. Under Alabama law providing for a jury trial to fix punishment on a guilty plea, the prosecution presented eye-witness testimony and petitioner's counsel cursorily cross-examined. Petitioner did not testify; no character or background testimony was presented for him; and there was nothing to indicate that he had a prior criminal record. The jury found petitioner guilty and sentenced him to death on each indictment. The Alabama Supreme Court reviewed the sentences under the State's automatic appeal statute for capital case, which requires the reviewing court to comb the record for prejudicial error even though not raised by counsel. Petitioner did not raise the question of the voluntariness of his guilty plea and the State Supreme Court did not pass on that question, though a majority of the court explicitly considered it in affirming his sentences of death.[25]

The defendant argued that a sentence of death for common-law robbery was cruel and unusual punishment within the meaning of the Federal Constitution. In their ruling, The Supreme Court of Alabama rejected this argument and affirmed the defendant's conviction. The case reached the United States Supreme Court, which reversed the defendant's conviction. It was held that "acceptance of the petitioner's guilty plea under the circumstances of this case constituted reversible error because the record does not disclose that the petitioner voluntarily and understandingly entered his plea of guilty."[26]

Delivering the judgment, Mr. Justice Douglas, stated that: "it was error, plain on the face of the record, for the trial judge to accept petitioner's guilty plea without an affirmative showing that it was intelligent and voluntary. That error, under Alabama procedure, was properly before the court below and considered explicitly by a majority of the justices and is properly before us on review."[27] Mr. Justice Douglas stated that:

> A plea of guilty is more than a confession which admits that the accused did various acts; it is itself a conviction; nothing remains but to give judgment and determine punishment. See Kercheval v. United States, 274 U.S. 220,223. Admissibility of a confession must be based on a "reliable determination on the voluntariness issue which satisfies the constitutional rights of the defendant." Jackson v. Denno, 378 U.S. 368, 387. The requirement that the prosecution spread on the record the prerequisites of a valid waiver is no constitutional innovation. In Carnley v. Cochran, 369 .U.S. 506, 516, we dealt with a problem of waiver of the right to counsel, a Sixth Amendment right. We held: "Presuming waiver from a silent record is impermissible. The record must show, or there must be an allegation and evidence which show, that an accused was offered counsel but intelligently and understandingly rejected the offer. Anything less is not waiver.[28]

In reversing the defendant's conviction, the Supreme Court also stated that "if a defendant's guilty plea is not voluntary and knowing, it has been obtained in violation of due process and is therefore void."[29] Furthermore, "because a guilty plea is an admission of all the elements of a formal criminal charge, it cannot be truly voluntary unless the defendant possesses an understanding of the law in relation to the facts."[30]

In *McCarthy v. United States*,[31] the United States Supreme Court granted certiorari to determine the proper construction of Rule 11 of the Federal Rules of Criminal Procedure and the effects of failure to adhere to the Rule by lower courts. In this case, the trial court accepted the defendant's guilty plea after the counsel stated that defendant fully understood the consequences of the plea. The defendant was convicted and he appealed his conviction arguing that the guilty plea should be set aside because the trial judge did not first address him personally to determine whether the plea was made voluntarily with an understanding of the nature of the charge and the consequences of the plea as required by Rule 11. In their ruling, The Court of Appeals affirmed the conviction and stated that the trial judge complied with Rule 11.[32]

The case reached the United States Supreme Court, which granted certiorari. The Supreme Court ruled that:

> (1) under Rule 11, the trial judge must personally inquire whether the defendant understood the nature of the charges against him, the Rule being designed to assist the district judge in making the constitutionally required determination that the guilty plea was truly voluntary, and to produce a complete record at the time of the plea of the factors relevant to such voluntariness determination; (2) any noncompliance with the Rule constituted reversible error, entitling the defendant to plead anew; and (3) the decision was made pursuant to the Supreme Court's

> supervisory power over the lower federal courts.[33]

Delivering the opinion of the United States Supreme Court, Chief Justice Warren said:

> Because of the importance of the proper construction of Rule 11 to the administration of criminal law in the federal courts, and because of a conflict in the courts of appeals over the effect of a district court's failure to follow the provisions of the Rule, we granted certiorari. We agree with petitioner that the District judge did not comply with Rule 11 in this case; and in reversing the Court of Appeals, we hold that a defendant is entitled to plead anew if a United States district court accepts his guilty plea without fully adhering to the procedure provided for in Rule 11. This decision is based solely upon our construction of Rule 11 and is made pursuant to our supervisory power over the lower federal courts; we do not reach any of the constitutional arguments petitioner urges as additional grounds for reversal.[34]

Chief Justice Warren also said Rule 11 requires the trial judge to inquire whether the defendant has an understanding of the nature of the charges and the consequences of the guilty plea. The judge must also ensure that there is a factual basis to the plea.[35] In reversing the judgment of the Court of Appeals, Chief Justice Warren said:

> We thus conclude that prejudice inheres in a failure to comply with Rule 11, for noncompliance deprives the defendant of the Rule's procedural safeguards that are designed to facilitate a more accurate determination of the voluntariness of his plea. Our holding that a defendant whose plea has been accepted in violation of Rule 11 should be afforded the opportunity to plead anew not only will insure that every accused is afforded those procedural

> safeguards, but also will help reduce the great waste of judicial resources required to process the frivolous attacks on guilty plea convictions that are encouraged, and are more difficult to dispose of, when the original record is inadequate. It is, therefore, not too much to require that, before sentencing defendants to years of imprisonment, district judges take the few minutes necessary to inform them of their rights and to determine whether they understand the action they are taking.[36]

The judgment of the Court of Appeals was reversed and the case was remanded for further proceedings.

Plea Bargaining must be Voluntary

There is also a requirement that the court must be satisfied that a defendant made the plea agreement voluntarily. This is the most contentious issue in the plea bargaining debate. Thus, in *Brady v. United States*,[37] the United States Supreme Court stated that, "the agents of the state may not produce a plea by actual or threatened physical harm or by mental coercion overbearing the will of the defendant."[38] In *Brady v. United States*,[39] the United States Supreme Court held that "to be admissible, a confession must be free and voluntary; that is, it must not be extracted by any sort of threats or violence, nor obtained by direct or implied promises, however slight, nor by the exertion of any improper influence."[40] In this case, the defendant argued that the death penalty of a statute made him decide to plead guilty. He contended that the guilty plea should therefore be set aside because it was coerced. The facts of the case are as follows:

> In 1959, the defendant entered a guilty plea under an indictment subjecting him to a maximum penalty of death for kidnapping under 18USC 1201(a), which makes the offense punishable by death only if the verdict of the jury so recommends. The defendant, represented throughout by competent counsel, originally had pleaded not guilty, but changed

his plea to guilty when a codefendant who had given a confession determined to plead guilty and became available to testify against the defendant. The trial judge twice questioned the defendant as to the voluntariness of his guilty plea before accepting it, and the defendant was sentenced to 50 years' imprisonment, later reduced to 30. In 1967, the defendant, acting under 28 USC 2255, sought relief in the United States District Court for the District of New Mexico, claiming that the death penalty provisions of 18 USC 1201(a) had operated to coerce his plea. The District Court, after a hearing, denied relief, holding that the statute was constitutional, and that in any event the guilty plea was voluntarily and knowingly made, the defendant having decided to plead guilty not because of the statute, but because of his codefendant's actions. On appeal, the Court of Appeals for the Tenth Circuit affirmed (404 F2d 601), holding that substantial evidence supported the finding that the guilty plea was voluntary, and concluding that a contrary result was not required by the intervening decision in United States v. Jackson (1968) 390 US 570, 20 L Ed 2d 138, 88 S Ct 1209, which held that the death penalty provision of the statute was unconstitutional as imposing an impermissible burden upon an accused's exercise of his Fifth Amendment right not to plead guilty and his Sixth Amendment right to demand trial by jury.[41]

The United States Supreme Court granted certiorari. The Supreme Court, through Mr. Justice White, stated that:

(1) The decision in *United States v. Jackson* did not require that every guilty plea entered under the statute be invalidated, even when the fear of death was shown to have been a factor in the plea.

(2) The voluntariness of a guilty plea under the statute was to be determined by considering all of the relevant circumstances, including the possibility of a heavier sentence following a guilty verdict.

(3) Even assuming that the defendant would not have pleaded guilty except for the death provision of the statute, nevertheless such assumption merely identified the penalty provision as a "but for" cause of his plea, and the fact that the statute caused the plea in such sense, did not necessarily prove that the plea was coerced and invalid as an involuntary act.

(4) A guilty plea was not invalid under the Fifth Amendment whenever it was motivated by the defendant's desire to accept the certainty or probability of a lesser penalty rather than face the possibility of a greater penalty after trial.

(5) The Fifth Amendment did not forbid prosecutors and judges to accept guilty pleas to selected counts, to lesser included offenses, or to reduced charges;

(6) A plea of guilty was not invalid merely because entered to avoid the possibility of a death penalty.

(7) The guilty plea in the case at bar was properly held to be valid as voluntarily and knowingly made, notwithstanding that the defendant might have been partially motivated by fear of the death penalty and notwithstanding that the death penalty provision of the statute was subsequently declared to be unconstitutional.[42]

The Supreme Court stated that the "agents of the state may not produce a plea of guilty by actual or threatened physical harm or by mental coercion overbearing the will of the defendant."[43] It was also held that "it does not violate the Fifth Amendment to influence or encourage a guilty plea by opportunity or promise of leniency, and a guilty plea is not coerced nor invalid merely because it was influenced by the fear of a possibly higher penalty for the crime charged if a conviction was obtained after the state was put to its proof." [44] In affirming Brady's conviction, Mr. Justice White said:

> The record before us also supports the conclusion that Brady's plea was intelligently made. He was advised by competent counsel, he was made aware of the nature of the charge against him, and there was nothing to indicate that he was incompetent or otherwise not in control of his mental faculties; once his confederate had pleaded guilty and became available to testify, he chosc to plead guilty, perhaps to ensure that he would face no more than life imprisonment or a term of years. Brady was aware of precisely what he was doing when he admitted that he had kidnapped the victim and had not released her unharmed.[45]

Knowing and Intelligent Plea

For a guilty plea to be valid, a defendant must also be made aware of the nature/elements of the charges, the minimum and maximum penalties and consequences of the plea agreement, and understand the significance of the rights that she is relinquishing. In *Henderson v. Morgan,*[46] the United States Supreme Court ruled that the guilty plea was constitutionally invalid because neither the defense attorney nor the prosecutor explained to the defendant the nature of the charge. The Court stated that intent was a "critical element" of the offense. In this case, it was held that "a plea may be involuntary either because the accused does not understand the nature of the constitutional protections that he is waiving, or because he has such an incomplete understanding of the charge that his plea cannot stand as an intelligent admission of guilt."[47]

The case involved a nineteen year old man who had a below average intelligence, who pleaded guilty to second degree murder but said that he "meant no harm" to the victim. Morgan was indicted with the first-degree murder of Mrs. Ada Francisco. Court records revealed that when Morgan was in the seventh grade, he was classified as "retarded" and sent to the Rome State School for Mental Defectives.[48] The court records also showed that:

> He was released to become a farm laborer and ultimately went to work on Mrs. Francisco's farm. Following an argument, she threatened to return him to state custody. He then decided to abscond. During the night he entered Mrs. Francisco's bedroom with a knife, intending to collect his earned wages before leaving; she awoke, began to scream, and he stabbed her. He took a small amount of money, fled in her car, and became involved in an accident about 80 miles away. The knife was found in the glove compartment of her car. He was promptly arrested and made a statement to the police. He was then 19 years old and substantially below average intelligence.[49]

Following a plea agreement and the advice of his attorneys, the defendant pleaded guilty to second-degree murder and was sentenced to an indeterminate term of imprisonment of 25 years to life.[50] The defendant filed a petition for a writ of habeas corpus after he had exhausted his state remedies. The defendant alleged that his guilty plea was involuntary, because he was not aware of the sentence that will be imposed if convicted of second-degree murder and also that he was not aware that intent to cause death was an element of the offense.[51] The United States District Court for the Northern District of New York ruled in favor of the petitioner. The Court of Appeals for the Second Circuit affirmed the district court's judgment.

The United States Supreme Court granted certiorari to determine "whether a defendant may enter a voluntary plea of guilty to a charge of second-degree murder without being informed that intent to cause death of his victim was an element of the offense."[52] It was held that:

> Since respondent did not receive adequate notice of the offense to which he pleaded guilty, his plea was involuntary and the judgment of conviction was entered without due process of law. The plea could not be voluntary in the sense that it constituted an intelligent admission that he committed the offense unless respondent received "real notice of the true nature of the charge against him, the first and most universally recognized requirement of due process." Smith v. O'Grady, 312 U.S. 329, 334. Where the record discloses that defense counsel did not purport to stipulate that respondent had the requisite intent or explain to him that his plea would be admission of that fact, and he made no factual statement or admission necessarily implying that he had such intent, it is impossible to conclude that his plea to the unexplained charge of second-degree murder was voluntary.[53]

In a footnote, the United States Supreme Court also stated that "there is no need in this case to decide whether notice of the true nature, or substance, of a charge always requires a description of every element of the offense; we assume it does not. Nevertheless, intent is such a critical element of the offense of second-degree murder that notice of that element is required."[54] Justice Stevens went on to say that:

> Normally the record contains either an explanation of the charge by the trial judge, or at least a representation by the defense counsel that the nature of the offense has been explained to the accused. Moreover, even without such an express representation, it may be appropriate to presume that in most cases defense counsel routinely explain the nature of the offense in sufficient detail to give the accused notice of what he is being asked to admit. This case is unique because the trial judge found as a fact that the element of intent

> was not explained to respondent. Moreover, respondent's unusually low mental capacity provides a reasonable explanation for counsel's oversight; it also forecloses the conclusion that the error was harmless beyond a reasonable doubt, for it lends at least a modicum of credibility to defense counsel's appraisal of the homicide as a manslaughter rather than a murder.[55]

In affirming the judgment of the Court of Appeals, Justice Stevens concluded that Morgan was not adequately made aware of the true nature/elements of the charges. Therefore, the guilty plea was entered involuntarily without due process of law.[56] The decision in *Henderson v. Morgan* was criticized. Joshua Dressler, for instance, contended that the decision is narrow, and seems to apply only to "undefined 'critical' elements of the crime."[57]

Competence

Another requirement that has to be satisfied before a plea bargain becomes valid relates to competence. Criminal defendants may not plead guilty, or waive counsel, unless they are mentally competent. The United States Supreme Court stated in *Godinez v. Moran*,[58] that the competency standard for pleading guilty or waiving the right to counsel is the same as the standard for competence to stand trial, namely, "whether the defendant has 'sufficient present ability to consult with his lawyer with a reasonable degree of rational understanding' and has 'a rational as well as factual understanding' of the proceedings against him."[59] The *Godinez* case involved a defendant who was charged with three counts of first degree murder. At first, he pleaded not guilty to the charges but later changed his plea to guilty after he dismissed his counsel.

Factual basis for the Plea

Finally, a plea bargain may be declared invalid unless there is a factual basis to the plea. The Federal Rules of Criminal Procedure, Rule 11, "requires the trial judge to determine that there is a factual basis for the defendant's guilty plea before entering a judgment on the plea." In a nutshell, if the court finds that there is no factual basis for the guilty plea, the court will reject the plea agreement.

1.4 HISTORICAL OVERVIEW

There is general disagreement amongst scholars as to the origin of plea bargaining. Some argue that it originated from England in the seventeenth century, while others argue that it started in America after the American Civil War. James E. Bond maintained that plea bargaining originated in seventeenth century England as a means of mitigating unduly harsh punishment.[60] On the other hand, Mary Vogel maintained that plea bargaining began in Boston around "the 1830s and 1840s as part of a process of political stabilization and an effort to legitimate institutions of self-rule."[61] She argued that an urban political elite in their quest to maintain power played a significant part in the introduction of plea bargaining, arguing that "it was this elite's perception of crises and threat, along with its effort to preserve social order, the legitimacy of self-rule and its own dominance, that produced in a single locale the practice of plea bargaining that would then become a national and, eventually international phenomenon."[62] Vogel concluded that there are three primary implications for the introduction of plea bargaining, and they are as follows:[63]

> First, what emerged was a powerful system of social control through the nonapplication of the law in ways that bore strong parallels to the British system of episodic leniency but with a uniquely American turn. Initially developed as part of a political project of protecting property, securing stability, and establishing popular consent, plea bargaining soon enhanced the discretionary power of both prosecutor and defense attorney.
>
> Second, plea bargaining, in its reliance on the Puritian confessional motif, reasserted a kind "fictive" secular community — the elite

> republican order that the Whigs struggled so mightily to sustain.
>
> Third, plea bargaining, through its use of intercessors, created links between the courts and employers that reinforced the workplace as a central element of societal social control in a way that would endure throughout the century. It integrated the courts with the powerful web of social control in everyday life. It is this third implication of plea bargaining that provides clues as to why the practice is so problematic today.[64]

A study of the work of the Superior Court of Alameda County in California between 1880 and 1910 concluded that plea bargaining was "used in Alameda County from at least 1880, though it was by no means as common in the late nineteenth century as it is today."[65] Hence, it has been argued that the development of plea bargaining could be connected with the structural and social changes in criminal justice, particularly the rise of professional police and prosecutors.[66]

One commentator argued that plea bargaining "did not occur with any frequency until well into the nineteenth century."[67] In fact four indications of plea bargaining prior to the American Civil War have been mentioned. The first is a "statute enacted in England, in 1485 that authorized the commencement of prosecutions for unlawful hunting before Justices of the Peace."[68] Under this statute, a defendant can be convicted of a summary offense if he confessed to having committed the crime or can be prosecuted as a felon if he denied committing the crime.[69] Albert Alschuler further maintained that "despite general disapproval, plea bargaining became a dominant method of resolving criminal cases at the end of the nineteenth century and at the beginning of the twentieth—at a time when the bondsman, the ward politician, the newspaper reporter, the jailer, and the fixer exerted an everyday influence on the administration of criminal justice."[70] He stated that in the 1920s, plea bargaining became a common practice but was met with disapproval from the general public.

It has been observed that five factors contributed to the development of contemporary plea bargaining: the complexity of criminal trial, urbanization, increased crime rates, expansion of the substantive criminal law, and the professionalization and increasing bureaucratization of the police, prosecution, and defense functions.[71] Alschuler noted that cases of plea bargaining started to appear in The United States appellate reports after the Civil War.[72] However, the first recorded case in the United States where guilty plea negotiation was addressed was in *Commonwealth v. Battis*.[73] The case involved a twenty year old man who was accused of raping and killing a thirteen year old girl. He broke her head with a stone and then threw her into the water. The accused pleaded guilty to the rape and murder. He was informed of the consequences of his guilty plea and also told that he was under no moral or legal obligation to plead guilty. He was also informed that he had the right to deny the charges and for the state to prove the case beyond a reasonable doubt. Under the circumstances, the court allowed him an extra day to give him the chance to consider his guilty plea. After the extra day, he again pleaded guilty to the charges. The court therefore, "examined, under oath, the sheriff, the jailer and justice, as to the sanity of the prisoner, and whether there had been tampering with him, either by promises, persuasions, or hopes of pardon if he would plead guilty."[74] Other cases in which guilty pleas were addressed during this period include *Swang v. State,*[75] *Wight v. Rindskpof,*[76] *Edwards v. People,*[77] and *State v. Richardson.*[78]

It should be noted, however, that the United States Supreme Court first addressed the issue of plea bargaining in *United States v. Jackson.*[79] In this case, the Supreme Court addressed the validity and constitutionality of plea bargaining. The Court was critical of a statute that allowed the imposition of the death penalty only after a trial by jury. In fact, the United States Supreme Court had to decide an appeal by the government asking for a review of the order of the United States District Court for the District of Connecticut, which "dismissed the kidnapping count of an indictment holding that the Federal Kidnapping Act was unconstitutional because it made 'the risk of death' the price for asserting the constitutional right to a jury trial."[80]

Delivering the judgment of the Supreme Court, Mr. Justice Stewart said that "the death penalty provision of the Federal Kidnapping Act imposes an impermissible burden upon the exercise of a constitutional right, but we think that provision is severable from the remainder of the statute."[81] The Supreme Court saw no reason to invalidate the entire Act. The United States Supreme Court stated that,

> Under the Federal Kidnapping Act, therefore, the defendant who abandons the right to contest his guilt before a jury is assured that he cannot be executed; the defendant ingenuous enough to seek a jury acquittal stands forewarned that, if the jury finds him guilty and does not wish to spare his life, he will die. Our problem is to decide whether the Constitution permits the establishment of such a death penalty, applicable only to those defendants who assert the right to contest their guilt before a jury. The inevitable effect of any such provision is, of course, to discourage assertion of the Fifth Amendment right not to plead guilty and to deter exercise of the Sixth Amendment right to demand a jury trial. If the provision had no other purpose or effect than to chill the assertion of constitutional rights by penalizing those who choose to exercise them, then it would be patently unconstitutional. But, as the Government notes, limiting the death penalty to cases where the jury recommends its imposition does have another objective: It avoids the more drastic alternative of mandatory capital punishment in every case. In this sense, the selective death penalty procedure established by the Federal Kidnapping Act may be viewed

> as ameliorating the severity of the more extreme punishment that Congress might have wished to provide.[82]

Justice Stewart went on to say that, "the evil in the federal statute is not that it necessarily coerces guilty pleas and jury waivers but simply that it needlessly encourages them. A procedure need not be inherently coercive in order that it be held to impose an impermissible burden upon the assertion of a constitutional right."[83] The judgment of the lower court was reversed and the case was remanded for further proceedings. In reversing the judgment, Mr. Justice Stewart said that, "By holding the death penalty clause of the Federal Kidnapping Act unenforceable, we leave the statute an operative whole, free of any constitutional objection. The appellees may be prosecuted for violating the Act, but they cannot be put to death under its authority."[84] The Supreme Court was right in this decision. There was no need to invalidate the Act in its entirety.

However, in *Brady v. United States*,[85] the United States Supreme Court reversed its position on plea bargaining. The Court stated that plea bargaining is not unconstitutional and that guilty pleas suggests some "hope for success in rehabilitation." The court also stated that the prior decision in *United States v. Jackson* merely required that guilty pleas be intelligent and voluntary. In *North Carolina v. Alford,*[86] the court abandoned the rehabilitation rationale for plea bargaining. In *North Carolina v. Alford,* the United States Supreme Court ruled that the trial judge did not commit constitutional error in accepting the defendant's plea, which was motivated by fear of the death penalty. In this case, Henry Alford was charged with first-degree murder in North Carolina in 1963. The North Carolina Law at the time provided for a sentence of life imprisonment for first-degree murder when the offender foregoes a trial and pleads guilty; death penalty was the sentence for first-degree if the defendant decides to go to trial and was convicted by the jury, unless the jury decides to recommend life imprisonment. There was penalty ranging from two to thirty years for second degree-murder. In this case, prosecutors had overwhelming evidence of the defendant's guilt. In fact,

> Appellee's attorney, in the face of strong evidence of guilt, recommended a guilty plea, but left the decision to appellee. The prosecutor agreed to accept a plea of guilty to second-degree murder. The trial court heard damaging evidence from certain witnesses before accepting a plea. Appellee pleaded guilty, although disclaiming guilt, because of the threat of the death penalty, and was sentenced to 30 years imprisonment. The Court of Appeals, on an appeal from a denial of a writ of habeas corpus, found that appellee's guilty plea was involuntary, because it was motivated principally by fear of the death penalty.[87]

Justice White, delivering the opinion of the United States Supreme Court, stated that the trial judge did not err by accepting the guilty plea. The judgment of the Court of Appeals was therefore reversed. Justice White said,

> Nor can we perceive any material difference between a plea that refuses to admit commission of the criminal act and a plea containing a protestation of innocence when, as in the instant case, a defendant intelligently concludes that his interests require entry of a guilty plea and the record before the judge contains strong evidence of actual guilt. Here the State had a strong case of first-degree murder against Alford. Whether he realized or disbelieved his guilt, he insisted on his plea because in his view he had absolutely nothing to gain by a trial and much to gain by pleading. Because of the overwhelming evidence against him, a trial was precisely what neither Alford nor his attorney desired. Confronted with the choice between a trial for first-degree murder, on the one hand, and a plea of guilty to second-degree murder, on the other hand, Alford quite reasonably chose the latter and thereby limited

> the maximum penalty to a 30-year term. When his plea is viewed in light of the evidence against him, which substantially negated his claim of innocence and which further provided a means by which the judge could test whether the plea was being intelligently entered, see McCarthy v. United States, supra, at 466-467 (1969), its validity cannot be seriously questioned. In view of the strong factual basis for the plea demonstrated by the State and Alford's clearly expressed desire to enter it despite his professed belief in his innocence, we hold that the trial judge did not commit constitutional error in accepting it.[88]

The Supreme Court ruled that the Court of Appeals for the Fourth Circuit erred in its ruling that Alford's guilty plea was involuntary because it was made to avoid the possibility of a death penalty.[89] Justice Brennan, Douglas and Marshall, JJ. dissented and stated that "the defendant's guilty plea was not voluntary, since the record showed that the plea was induced by the influence of the unconstitutional threat of the death penalty, the defendant's denial of guilt also being a relevant factor in determining whether the plea was voluntarily and intelligently made."[90]

Later in *Santobello v. New York*,[91] the United States Supreme Court also ruled that plea bargaining is not unconstitutional. The court stated that "the disposition of criminal charges by agreement between the prosecutor and the accused, sometimes loosely called 'plea bargaining' is an essential component of the administration of justice. Properly administrated, it is to be encouraged."[92] Justice Burger, delivering the opinion of the court, stated the following:

> Disposition of charges after plea discussions is not only an essential part of the process but a highly desirable part for many reasons. It leads to prompt and largely final disposition of most criminal cases; it avoids much of the corrosive

> impact of enforced idleness during pre-trial confinement for those who are denied release pending trial; it protects the public from those accused persons who are prone to continue criminal conduct even while on pretrial release; and, by shortening the time between charge and disposition, it enhances whatever may be the rehabilitative prospects of the guilty when they are ultimately imprisoned.[93]

Chief Justice Burger further stated that plea bargaining is to be encouraged because, "if every criminal charge were subjected to a full-scale trial, the States and the Federal Government would need to multiply by many times the number of judges and court facilities."[94]

At this point, it should be noted that in 1967 the America Bar Association recognized and accepted plea bargaining. Similarly, the President's Commission on Law Enforcement and Administration of Justice also approved plea bargaining in 1967. In 1973, however, the National Advisory Commission on Criminal Justice Standards and Goals called for the abolition of plea bargaining. The Commission maintained that plea bargaining should be abolished "as soon as possible, but no event later than 1978, negotiations between prosecutors and defendants either personally or through their attorneys, concerning concessions to be made in return for guilty pleas should be abolished." It should be noted that this recommendation was not carried out. However, it did trigger a great number of calls for the abolition of plea bargaining.

It is noteworthy to point out that there have been several attempts to ban plea bargaining in The United States. Alaska was the first state to ban plea bargaining. In 1975, Alaska's Attorney General banned plea bargaining in the state, arguing that the ban would ensure fairness, restore public confidence in the criminal justice system, and improve the trial skills of his prosecutorial staff. The ban lasted for ten years. In 1978 the El Paso County in Texas also banned plea bargaining. The ban was initiated to ensure sentence uniformity, but it was only in effect for six years. This was followed by an attempt to ban plea bargaining in California. In 1982 voters in California approved a referendum to ban plea bargaining in serious felonies and "other enumerated crimes." The statute prohibits plea bargaining in a serious felony, a felony in which the accused used a firearm, or any offense of driving while under the influence of alcohol or any drug. It also permits plea bargaining if the evidence is inadequate to prove the charge, the testimony of a material witness cannot be obtained, or the negotiated settlement does not result in a substantial change in the sentence. Plea bargaining is still practiced in California today.

In 1992, the Bronx County in New York banned plea bargaining in indicted felony cases. The District Attorney, Robert Johnson, maintained that no plea bargaining would be allowed after a defendant has been indicted by a grand jury. The ban was criticized.[95]

From the above discussion, one can safely say that plea bargaining was practiced in England before it began in The United States. It is also safe to say that plea bargaining did not originate as a result of crowded court cases. As Freidman has pointed out, in Alameda County of California, "the population of the county was about 60,000 in 1880 and the felony caseload was small—about 100 cases a year in the 1880s."[96]

1.5 ADVANTAGES AND DISADVANTAGES OF PLEA BARGAINING

Plea bargaining is a process that has generated a lot of controversy. However, one thing is clear, and that is the fact that all the participants in this process derive some benefits from it.

Advantages to the Defendant

The first and major advantage that a defendant derives from plea bargaining is that he gets a lesser sentence and also gets a dismissal of some charges. Thus, defendants escape getting the maximum punishment prescribed by law. Second, under plea bargaining, the uncertainty of trial outcome is removed. Obviously, a trial before a jury of twelve people or before a judge is simply unpredictable. By agreeing to a plea bargain, the defendant knows straight away what the sentence is. There is also the advantage of having a speedy and final disposition of the case. Allied to the above, is the fact that the anxiety of going through a trial is removed. A defendant does not have to go through the strains and stresses involved with a trial. Furthermore, the case is disposed of quickly. Plea bargaining is quicker than going to a trial, which involves many court dates, adjournments and so on. One of the main reasons why some defendants decide to forego a court trial is because they think that judges might impose more severe sentences once the judges hear full details of the cases from the victims. Judge R. A. Fine noted a case where a defense lawyer told him "on the record that he was removing his client's case from my court because he had worked out a "great plea bargain" with the prosecutor, which he did not think I would accept. When I asked for specifics, he replied that he did not want to tell me the deal because "you'd be so grossed out."[97] Judge Fine concluded that plea bargaining should be abolished, because it encourages crime and demoralizes both the victim and the society.[98] He maintained that "we short change our citizens when we settle for a criminal justice system that gives them much crime but little justice. The expediency-based practice of plea bargaining has done precisely that. Our people deserve better."[99]

In some cases, the defendant also avoids a pre-trial detention if they agree to a plea bargain and it is approved by the court. It should also be noted that by pleading guilty straight away, the defendant also saves the cost of hiring a private attorney. The cost will be higher if a defendant chooses to go for a trial.

Plea bargaining helps a defendant avoid publicity, especially in cases with stigma. Imagine a high profile politician who was arrested for soliciting prostitutes. The secretive nature of plea bargaining, therefore, benefits the accused who does not want the general public to know about his offense. In fact, it has been noted that a defendant's background is rarely explored during plea bargaining as opposed to the extent that it may be explored if there is a trial.[100]

A defendant also benefits from plea bargaining by having a less serious offense entered in his criminal record. For instance, a defendant can plead guilty to a misdemeanor rather than risk going to trial where he may be convicted of a felony. Hence, it is no surprise that in 1974 in New York, 80 percent of felony cases were settled through plea bargaining as misdemeanors and two percent of felony cases went to trial.[101]

Disadvantages of Plea Bargaining to a Defendant

The main disadvantage of plea bargaining to a defendant is that plea bargaining is coercive in nature. It tends to coerce innocent defendants to plead guilty. Plea bargaining puts enormous pressure on defendants to plead guilty, and in the words of Professor Schulhofer:

> The major problem with plea bargaining is that it forces the party into a situation where they have to take a guess about what the evidence is, about how strong the case might be, and they have to make that guess against the background of enormously severe penalties if you guess wrong. So defendants, even if they are innocent, in fact face enormous pressure to play the odds and to accept a plea. And the more likely they are to be innocent, and the stronger their defenses are, the bigger the discount and the bigger benefits the prosecutor will offer them. Eventually at some point it becomes so tempting that it might be irresistible, especially when the consequences of guessing wrong are disastrous.[102]

Another disadvantage of plea bargaining is that a defendant relinquishes some of his constitutional rights, such as the right to trial by jury. Furthermore, under plea bargaining, a defendant gets convicted even without any evidence. The evidence against the defendant (if any) are not heard or contested by the due process. Above all, a defendant who enters a plea bargain forfeits any chance of acquittal at trial.

Advantages and Disadvantages of Plea Bargaining to a Prosecutor

Prosecutors also derive a lot of benefits from plea bargaining. Prosecutors do not have to prove a case to secure a conviction. In fact, "when plea bargaining is available, prosecutors can extract a guilty plea in nearly every case, including very weak cases, simply by adjusting the plea concession to the defendant's chances of acquittal at trial."[103] Under plea bargaining, prosecutors do not seem to be interested in screening away weak cases; as a result, more innocent defendants are charged and convicted without strong evidence.[104]

The main point is that under plea bargaining, prosecutors do not face the risk of losing cases where there is insufficient evidence. In cases where there is insufficient evidence linking the defendant to the offenses charged, the prosecutor will resort to plea bargaining. Many of the accused persons are therefore convicted on less than the standard of proof. Prosecutors like plea bargaining because they do not have to prepare a case and prove the case beyond a reasonable doubt before a judge or jury. Hence, prosecutors and courts see guilty pleas as a convenient, efficient and reliable method of disposing cases.[105]

Furthermore, under plea bargaining, prosecutors obtain guilty pleas without going to trial, thereby saving time and money. The pressure of going to trial is also removed. Prosecutors are also able to deal with more cases. Plea bargaining enables them to deal with cases quickly taking only minutes, while trials can last weeks, months, or years.

The main disadvantage of plea bargaining to the prosecutors is that it tends to make them lazy. In fact,

"Plea bargaining provides extraordinary opportunities for lazy lawyers whose primary goal is to cut corners and get on to the next case."[106] Defense attorneys also become lazy as a result, and neither side develops trial skills.

Advantages and Disadvantages to the Defense Counsel

The main advantage of plea bargaining to the defense counsel is that it ensures a quick disposal of cases. It reduces caseloads. A defense counsel can deal with a large number of clients as there is no preparation for trial. Plea barraging also saves defense attorneys' money and the time needed for trial preparation. And as Gerald Robin has pointed out, "By staying out of courtrooms, private attorneys stay in business."[107]

The main disadvantage of plea bargaining to defense attorneys is that it creates a dilemma for them. Here, the defense attorney knows that his or her client is innocent; the case is weak; there is a good chance of winning at trial, but you are faced with the dilemma that if you lose, your client will go to prison. This is one of the evils and disadvantages of plea bargaining.

Advantages and Disadvantages to Judges

Plea bargaining undoubtedly reduces the caseloads of judges. It saves them time and resources. There is speedy disposition of a large number of cases. Plea bargaining also helps judges to avoid the stresses and problems involved with conducting a trial. For instance, the danger of having found to have erred in their judgment is removed.

The main disadvantage of plea bargaining to judges is that it undermines their status. Indeed, Chad Baruch maintained that "plea bargaining also transforms judges from respected arbiters of justice to mere paper-pushing figureheads who "bless" transactions already negotiated among counsel."[108]

Advantages of Plea Bargaining to Victims

Plea bargaining saves the victims the stresses and rigors of going through a trial. It also saves them time as they do not have to go to court to testify. Above all, victims may get a quick sense of closure that the offender is being punished for the crime, that is, if the sentence was acceptable to the victim, which is rare.

Advantages and Disadvantages to the Society

The main benefit to the society is that it saves time and money. There is the idea that it is too expensive to try every case. There are no witnesses to call, no jurors needed. People do not have to leave their jobs to serve as jurors. The time lag between the offense and the punishment is also reduced.[109]

The main disadvantage to the society is that there is no public hearing and the public does not get to see any trial. Plea bargaining is secretive.

In spite of the disadvantages of plea bargaining, it seems acceptable to some people, especially in European countries, when it is used in minor cases. In France, plea bargaining was introduced in 2004, and used mainly in misdemeanors and felony offenses that carry maximum sentences of up to five years imprisonment. The French plea bargaining, which was basically introduced to reduce caseloads and solve overcrowding in prisons, authorizes the prosecutor to recommend one-year maximum sentence for defendants who plead guilty or nolo contendere to the charges.

General Disadvantages of Plea Bargaining

One commentator pointed out correctly that something is seriously wrong with a criminal justice system where lawyers avoid the due process model as if it is a plague; where cases are decided based on administrative conveniences, and where sentences given are unrelated to the offenses or the correctional needs of the offenders.[110] Robin has done considerable work outlining some of the general disadvantages of plea bargaining and some of them are as follows:[111]

1. Research has shown that plea bargaining is demoralizing to the police and a source of

friction with the prosecutor, who relies on the police as an investigative arm in cases that go to trial.

2. Because of plea bargaining, defendants who should be confined longer are not, and defendants who should be released are incarcerated. Offenders are disposed of undeterred, untreated, and with minimal regard for public safety.
3. Plea bargaining undermines the basic premise of "crime and punishment" that is the foundation of the criminal law and the criminal justice system.
4. Plea bargaining is an infringement on the court's responsibility and discretion in sentencing.
5. Plea bargaining makes the preparation of presentence reports by probation officers a wasted effort, because the sentence has already been negotiated. When presentence reports are ignored, sentences have minimal correctional or punitive value. Indeed, the information disclosed in the presentence report may cast doubt on the wisdom of the plea bargain (which the state must nevertheless exercise in good faith to avoid the accusation of broken promises).
6. Bargain-basement justice is always more of a bargain for the defendant than it is for the state and the public. If the defendant does simply hold out for trial, knowing that the legal strength of the state's case will be weakened further by time.
7. Plea bargaining provides the opportunity for defense counsel (and prosecutors) to place their own economic and occupational needs ahead of the fundamental interests of their clients.[112]

1.6 CONCERNS AND CRITICISMS OF PLEA BARGAINING

Plea bargaining is a process that is fundamentally flawed and raises a lot of concerns. It is a process that coerces innocent defendants to plead guilty without giving them the chance of an acquittal. As Judge Easterbrook has pointed out, "a perfect system entails no guilty pleas by innocent persons"[113] Furthermore, in most cases, there are many pressures on prosecutors and defense attorneys, which may lead to injustice.[114] Hence, "plea bargaining has become the norm and the trial an anomaly."[115] In a similar vein, Kenneth Kipnis maintained that our criminal justice system is not operating as it should arguing that, "the conviction secured through jury trial, so familiar in countless novels, films, and television programs, is beginning to be seen as the aberration it has become."[116]

One of the major concerns about plea bargaining is that too much power is being exercised by the prosecutor. Under plea bargaining, the accusatory, determinative, and sanctional phases are all placed under the prosecutor.[117] Hence, one commentator described plea bargaining as a process of prosecutorial tyranny.[118] Langbein further maintained that there "is a very evil interaction of prosecutorial power with poverty, with indigence,"[119] arguing that the majority of the people suffering within the system are poor people.[120] Rich people tend to get the full trials.[121]

Plea bargaining has also been seen to be "rife with unfair prosecutorial tactics."[122] Plea bargaining can be abused by prosecutors. In fact, Timothy Sandefur observed that, "prosecutors know how to exploit limits on habeas corpus rights, mandatory sentencing rules, and loopholes that allow evidence collected under questionable circumstances to be admitted."[123]

The coercive nature of plea bargaining is another main concern and criticism leveled against plea bargaining. Plea bargaining leads innocent defendants to plead guilty. In fact, Alschuler maintained that plea bargaining "is marvelously designed to secure the conviction of the innocent."[124] Plea bargaining makes it advantageous for innocent defendants to plead guilty.[125] Furthermore, plea bargaining "systematically confronts them with offers calculated to overbalance their chances of acquittal. Blocking defendants from declaring in public, 'I didn't do it, but I want to take the deal,' does not send a moral message. It only increases the system's hypocrisy."[126]

It has been argued that under plea bargaining criminal sanctions are given out without adjudication.[127] Another great concern regarding the practice of plea bargaining is that the process is so speedy that the effectiveness, thoroughness, and the procedure becomes questionable. Professors Robert Scott and William Stuntz would support this view and they wrote:

> Most cases are scandalously casual: a quick conversation at a prosecutor's office or courthouse hallway between attorneys familiar with only the basics of the case, with no witnesses present, leading to a proposed resolution that is then 'sold' to both the defendant and the judge. To a large extent, this kind of horse trading determines who goes to jail and for how long. That is what plea bargaining is. It is not some adjunct to the criminal justice system; it is the criminal justice system.[128]

Another argument against plea bargaining is that it adversely affects the quality of legal representation defense attorneys provide for their clients.[129] There are several advantages that defense attorneys derive from plea bargaining and these can blur their decision whether to advise their clients to plead guilty or go to trial. Mark Cammack and Norman Garland noted that sometimes defense attorneys may agree to a plea deal so that they do not jeopardize their ongoing relationship with some prosecutors.[130] Furthermore, defense attorneys may feel tempted to recommend pleading guilty, because it involves less risk to the lawyer's reputation.[131]

As mentioned earlier, under plea bargaining prosecutors and defense attorneys do not develop trial skills. As a result the skills of good advocacy are lost. The criminal justice system becomes weak because we do not have skilled advocates. This arguably leads prosecutors into becoming meaningless bureaucrats.

In two recent cases, the United States Supreme Court touched on the issue of the consequences of bad legal advice during plea bargaining. In *Missouri v. Frye,*[132] and *Lafler v. Cooper,*[133] the Supreme Court stated that in cases where ineffective defense representation caused a defendant to reject a favorable plea bargain, that the defendant has the right to a second trial. In *Missouri v. Frye,* the defendant's lawyer failed to inform him of a plea offer by the prosecutor. After the offer expired, the defendant pleaded guilty without the plea deal. He was convicted and sentenced to three years imprisonment. In this case, the defendant, Galin E. Frye was charged with driving with a revoked license. He has been convicted of this offense on three other occasions, and the prosecutor sent a letter to Frye's attorney offering him two plea bargains with an expiration date. Frye filed for post-conviction relief and alleged that his "counsel's failure to inform him of the prosecutor's plea offer denied him the effective assistance of counsel."[134] He stated that he would have accepted the plea offer of a misdemeanor charge if he had been informed of the offer. The state court denied the post-conviction motion. The defendant appealed and the case reached the United States Supreme Court, which stated that the Fourteenth Amendment "provides that the accused shall have the assistance of counsel in all criminal prosecutions. The right to counsel is the right to effective assistance of counsel."[135] Delivering the opinion of the Supreme Court, Mr. Justice Kennedy said:

> This Court now holds that, as a general rule, defense counsel has the duty to communicate formal offers from the prosecution to accept a plea on terms and conditions that may be favorable to the accused. Any exceptions to that rule need not be explored here, for the offer was

> a formal one with a fixed expiration date. When defense counsel allowed the offer to expire without advising the defendant or allowing him to consider it, defense counsel did not render the effective assistance the Constitution requires.[136]

The decision of the Missouri Court of Appeals was therefore vacated and the case was remanded for further proceedings.

Plea bargaining is also seen as a practice that devalues human liberty "by viewing it as a commodity to be traded for economic and time saving purposes and in doing so, it undermines the sanctity of the judicial process."[137] It has also been noted that plea bargaining seriously impairs the public interest in effective punishment of crime and in accurate separation of the guilty from the innocent.[138] Schulhofer maintained that plea bargaining is a disaster, arguing that:

> With trials in open court and deserved sentences imposed by a neutral fact finder, we protect the due process right to an adversarial trial, minimize the risk of unjust conviction of the innocent, and at the same time further the public interest in effective law enforcement and adequate punishment of the guilty. But plea negotiation simultaneously undercuts all of these interests. The affected parties are represented by agents who have inadequate incentives for proper performance; prospects for effective monitoring are limited or nonexistent; and the dynamics of negotiation can create irresistible pressure for defendants to falsely condemn themselves. As a result, plea agreements defeat the public interest in effective law enforcement at the same time they deny defendants the benefits of a vigorous defense and inflict undeserved punishment on innocents who could win acquittal at trial.[139]

Similarly, Alschuler argued that plea bargaining makes figurehead of judges; has transferred judges' powers to lawyers who now see themselves as judges and administrators, and "whose temperaments have been shaped by their partisan duties, and who have not been charged by the electorate with the important responsibilities that they have assumed."[140]

Plea bargaining has also been criticized because it results in sentence disparity. There is ample evidence that defendants who plead guilty receive more lenient sentences than defendants who are convicted at trial.[141] The question is—why should a defendant get a lesser sentence just for acknowledging that he or she committed a crime? Indeed, "the sentencing disparity reflects the necessity of offering the defendant an inducement to forego the possibility of an acquittal and plead guilty."[142] Plea bargaining, therefore, "inevitably produces the ridiculous result that as crime grows worse, sentencing becomes more lenient. Plea negotiations arose and persist for the purpose of expediting the cases, the prosecutors have to offer progressively better deals."[143] In the end, a defendant who asked for trial gets a harsher sentence. Therein lies one of the evils of plea bargaining.

In *Bordenkircher v. Hayes*,[144] Paul Lewis Hayes was indicted by the grand jury on a charge of uttering a forged check of $88.30. The State of Kentucky statute at the time of the offense stated that the offense carries a prison term of two to ten years. The prosecutor offered Hayes a plea deal whereby Hayes will plead guilty to the offense, and in exchange the prosecutor offered to recommend a sentence of five years. The prosecutor also said that "if Hayes did not plead guilty and "saved the court the inconvenience and necessity of a trial," he would return to the grand jury to seek an indictment under the Kentucky Habitual Criminal Act, which would subject Hayes to a mandatory sentence of life imprisonment by reason of his two prior felony convictions."[145] Hayes decided not to plead guilty and was charged under the Habitual Criminal Act. Hayes was convicted by the jury, and based on his two prior felonies he was sentenced to mandatory life imprisonment. Hayes petitioned for a writ of habeas corpus. The United States District Court for the Eastern District of Kentucky denied the writ, and ruled that the indictment procedure and the sentence were constitutional. Hayes appealed his conviction and sentence. The Court of Appeals ruled in Hayes' favor and reversed the district court's decision. The Court of Appeals for the Sixth Circuit stated that Hayes' due process rights were violated when he was reindicted, convicted, and sentenced for a more serious charge because of his refusal to plead guilty to the original lesser charge.[146] The case went to the United States Supreme Court for review.[147] In their ruling, the United States Supreme Court reversed the decision of the Court of Appeals and stated that, "The due process clause of the Fourteenth Amendment is not violated when a state prosecutor carries out a threat made during plea negotiations to have the accused reindicted on more serious charges on which he is plainly subject to prosecution if he does not plead guilty to the offense with which he was originally charged."[148]

Mr. Justice Harry Blackmun, who was joined in his dissent by Brennan and Marshall, JJ., was of the view that prosecutorial vindictiveness was present in this case and he wrote:

> The Court now says, however, that this concern with vindictiveness is of no import in the present case, despite the difference between five years in prison and a life sentence, because we are here concerned with plea bargaining where there is give-and-take negotiation, and where, it is said, "there is no such element of punishment or retaliation so long as the accused is free to accept or reject the prosecution's offer." Yet in this case vindictiveness is present to the same extent as it was thought to be in *Pearce* and in *Perry;* the prosecutor here admitted, that the sole reason for the new indictment was to discourage the respondent from exercising his right to a trial.

> Even had such an admission not been made, when plea negotiations, conducted in the face of the less serious charge under the first indictment, fail, charging by a second indictment a more serious crime for the same conduct creates "a strong inference" of vindictiveness. As then Judge McCree aptly observed, in writing for a unanimous panel of the Sixth Circuit, the prosecutor initially "makes a discretionary determination that the interests of the state are served by not seeking more serious charges." *Hayes v. Cowan,* 547 F. 2d 42, 44 (1976). I therefore do not understand why, as in *Pearce*, due process does not require that the prosecution justify its action on some basis other than discouraging respondent from the exercise of his right to a trial.[149]

Justice Blackmun went on to say that the Due Process Clause ought to protect defendants against prosecutorial vindictiveness.[150] Mr. Justice Powell also dissented and stated that although he agreed with much of the majority opinion that he was "not satisfied that the result in this case is just or that the conduct of the plea bargaining met the requirements of due process."[151] Justice Powell further stated that "in this case, the prosecutor's actions denied respondent due process, because their admitted purpose was to discourage and then to penalize with unique severity his exercise of constitutional rights. Implementation of a strategy calculated solely to deter the exercise of constitutional rights is not constitutionally permissible exercise of discretion."[152] This case has clearly shown the shortcomings of plea bargaining. Here we have seen a classic example of prosecutorial tyranny, the coercive nature of plea bargaining and the fact that plea bargaining is all about threat and nothing but the threat. Plea bargaining is ridiculous and should be abolished.

Plea bargaining has been described as a double evil that "encourages crime by weakening the credibility of the system on the one hand and, on the other, it tends to extort guilty pleas from the innocent."[153] Judge Fine argued that the idea that the criminal justice system will collapse without plea bargaining is just a myth.[154] He noted that the leniency that a defendant gets by pleading guilty is nothing but a payment to the defendant so that he forgoes a trial.[155] How do we explain cases where someone with a documented history of sexual abuse, molests his five-year-old daughter, and was charged with child molestation, but the prosecutor decides to offer him a plea deal whereby the charge is reduced to Lewd and Lascivious Conduct with a Child under 14.[156] In fact, "charging a rape as 'disorderly conduct,' for example, under the aegis of a 'half a loaf is better than none' theory, disables justice as the victim wonders, and the criminal gloats at the law's impotence."[157]

Another concern about plea bargaining relates to the issue of whether statements made during plea discussions (omnibus hearings) should be admissible at later trial, where it is believed that the defendant did not intend to enter into a guilty plea. This issue was addressed by the Court of Appeals of Minnesota in *State v. Brown*,[158] where it was held that a court can decline to "apply Rule 410's protections to statements that involve neither an offer to plea guilty nor a bargained confession."[159] In this case, the defendant argued that the admission of the statements by Hennepin County District Court violated Minn. R. Evid. 410. Rule 410 states that "Except as otherwise provided in this rule, evidence of the following is not, in any civil or criminal proceeding, admissible against the defendant who made the plea or was a participant in the discussions:

(1) a plea of guilty, which was later withdrawn;
(2) a plea of nolo contendere;
(3) any statement made in the course of any proceedings under Rule 11 of the Federal Rules of Criminal Procedure or comparable state procedure regarding either of the forgoing pleas; or
(4) any statements made in the course of plea discussions with an attorney for the prosecuting authority, which do not result in a plea of guilty or which result in a plea of guilty later withdrawn."

However, such a statement is admissible (i) in any proceeding wherein another statement made in the course of the same plea or plea discussion has been introduced and the statement ought in fairness be considered contemporaneously with it, or (ii) in a criminal proceeding for perjury or false statement if the statement was made by the defendant under oath, on the record, and in the presence of counsel.[160]

This case involved Adolphus Brown, who was charged with attempted second-degree murder and possession of a pistol without a permit.[161] At the omnibus hearing, he stated that he had a permit for the gun. During the omnibus hearing, Brown said: "I'm looking forward to the truth coming out. That's why we're going to trial."[162] Following this statement, the prosecutor decided to withdraw the plea offer and proceeded to set the case for trial. At the trial, Brown pleaded not guilty. He contended that he fired the gun in self-defense and to defend others. On cross-examination, Brown admitted he did not have a permit for the gun. He stated that "he thought he had applied and received a permit."[163]

The jury convicted Brown of attempted second-degree murder and for possession of a gun without permit. He appealed his conviction, arguing that the admission of evidence of his omnibus hearing statements by the trial court was error because the statements were inadmissible under Minn. R. Evid. 410.[164] In its ruling, the Court of Appeals of Minnesota stated that:

> The fact that an appellant's statements are made in response to a plea offer tendered by the State is not dispositive. The policy underlying Minn. R. Evid. 410 does not support exclusion of every statement made in response to a tendered plea offer, or in a typical plea-negotiation context, without regard to the defendant's subjective expectation. The policy is as follows: In general, the court recognizes that plea bargains are essential to the administration of justice. With proper

> safeguards, pleas should be a most frequent means for the disposition of criminal cases. The purpose of Rule 410 is to encourage frank discussion in plea bargaining negotiations. In order to further this policy and ensure fruitful negotiations, Rule 410 safeguards the confidentiality of plea negotiations by precluding the evidentiary use of plea-related statements in the event that plea negotiations abort. Meaningful dialogue between the parties will, as a practical matter, be impossible if either party has to assume the risk that plea offers will be admissible in evidence.[165]

The Court went on to say that "cases are not disposed of through plea bargaining unless the defendant offers to plead guilty or at the very least exhibits an actual subjective expectation to negotiate a plea."[166] Justice Michelle A. Larkin, delivering the opinion of the Court of Appeals, said:

> We hold that statements made by a defendant that are not part of a guilty plea or an offer to plead guilty are admissible under Minn. R. Evid. 410 unless the defendant exhibited an actual subjective expectation to negotiate a plea when statements were made and the expectation was reasonable, given the totality of the objective circumstances. Because the appellant did not exhibit an actual subjective expectation to negotiate a plea when he made his omnibus-hearing statements, we conclude that the district court did not err by admitting evidence of the statements at trial. We also conclude that the evidence was sufficient to support appellant's conviction and that appellant waived his pro se claim regarding lesser-included jury instructions. We therefore affirm.[167]

The case reached the Supreme Court of Minnesota, which on January 5, 2011 reversed the Court of Appeals decision and remanded for a new trial. It was held that the admission of Brown's omnibus-hearing statement was plain error. Therefore his conviction had to be reversed. Delivering the opinion of the Court, Justice Barry G. Anderson stated that:

> The district court allowed the State to cross-examine Brown about statements he made in connection with the State's offer to resolve the pending criminal charges, in open court, and in response to questioning by the court itself. Allowing the use of such evidence at trial undermines the purpose and language of Minn. R. Evid. 410 and calls into question the fairness and integrity of the judicial proceeding against Brown. A new trail on the second-degree attempted murder is therefore necessary.[168]

Another case worth mentioning is the unusual, bizarre, and ridiculous plea agreement involving Tremayne Durham, age 33, from New York City. The facts of the case are that in June 2006, Adam Calbreath, age 39, from Gresham, was shot to death in Portland, Oregon. Durham bought an ice cream truck for $18,000 from an Oregon company where the victim worked at the time. He wanted to use the truck to start his own ice cream business, but he later changed his mind and asked for a refund. He was informed that the company will not issue a refund. He therefore, travelled from New York to Oregon, and it was then that he shot Calbreath.

Durham was arrested for the murder. He confessed to the murder and asked for Kentucky Fried Chicken, calzones and pizza in exchange for a guilty plea to the murder. It was reported that Durham was serving a two-year jail term at Multnomah County jail and wanted a better meal. Durham is a convicted rapist. "Durham agreed to plead guilty to murder, but only if he could get a break from jail food. The judge agreed and granted Durham a feast of KFC chicken, Popeye's chicken, mashed potatoes, coleslaw, carrot cake and ice cream."[169] At Multnomah County Court, the trial judge agreed to the plea deal.

Under the plea deal, it was agreed that Durham will be sentenced to life in prison, but with the possibility of parole after 30 years. Without the plea deal, Durham could be facing a death sentence of life in prison without the possibility of parole, if convicted by the jury. And there was abundant evidence to convict him if he had gone to trial. Durham has a long history of serious crimes. It was reported that he faked a suicide, choked a fellow inmate as well as threats to a jail van.[170] Here is a case of a convicted rapist and murderer being given a lesser sentence. Most likely, he will be released after 30 years only to come back to the community to commit further gruesome crimes. It should be noted that, "as part of the plea deal, Durham also asked to serve his sentence in a New York prison. Although Oregon doesn't have an interstate compact with New York, Judge Bergstrom said he'd write a letter asking that Durham be transferred to a prison nearby, perhaps in New Jersey or Connecticut."[171] In who's best interest is this plea deal? Deputy District Attorney Josh Lamborn believed that this plea deal will save the costs of a full jury trial. The key question is: Is this a mockery of the system? This plea deal is ethically and morally suspect. Plea bargaining is a ridiculous practice that serves the best interest of a guilty defendant. Commenting on this plea deal, Judge Michael McShane maintained that "judges sometimes have to be flexible in negotiating plea deals. Even if a chicken dinner seems like caving to the whims of a killer, it's really an inconsequential concession in the long run for a death-penalty case."[172]

In another unusual plea bargaining case, a court approved a plea deal after a defendant had been convicted by a jury. The case involved Hans Thomas Reiser, a computer programmer, from Oakland, California, who was charged with the murder of his wife, Nina Reiser. On September 5, 2006, Nina was reported missing. The last time she was seen alive was on September 3, 2006 when she dropped off her two children at her mother-in law's house where her estranged husband was living at the time. The Reisers got married in 1999 but separated in 2004 following several marital problems.

Following police investigations, Hans Reiser was a suspect in his wife's disappearance. In October 2006 Reiser was formally arrested for the murder of his wife. Evidence gathered by the police, even though they were circumstantial, were enough for the police to conclude that Reiser murdered his wife. Blood splatters were found in Reiser's car. The passenger seat of Reiser's car was missing after Nina's disappearance. Reiser was also seen washing 'something' off his driveway after Nina's disappearance. Police also found two books on murder investigations, which Reiser reportedly bought five days after Nina's disappearance. Furthermore, Nina's blood was found on a pillar at the house where Reiser was staying (his mother's house). Based on the above details, Reiser was charged with first-degree murder of Nina.

In March 2007, he pleaded not guilty. During the trial, Reiser denied any knowledge of Nina's murder. It was reported that Reiser was offered a plea deal by the prosecutor whereby he will plead guilty to voluntary manslaughter and in exchange he will be sentenced to the minimum prison term of three years. The maximum prison term is 11 years. If convicted by a jury, first-degree murder charge carries a sentence of 25 years to life. Reiser apparently refused this plea offer. In fact, the judge said he would have approved the plea deal because it would have saved the tax payers the cost of the trial, spared Reiser's eight-year-old son from testifying in court, and also bring some sort of closure to Nina's family and friends.[173] The question is—are these acceptable reasons to enter into a plea deal with a calculated and cold-blooded killer, who carried on lying and denying any knowledge of his wife's disappearance and murder? Who benefits ultimately from this sort of deal? Why should a cold-blooded killer be given only three years imprisonment by simply pleading guilty to an offense lesser than the one actually committed?

The jury on April 28, 2008, convicted Reiser of the first-degree murder of Nina. Judge Larry Goodman presided over the trial. The sentencing date was scheduled. In a bizarre and unusual twist, the prosecutor offered Reiser a new deal, whereby Reiser will tell the authorities how he killed Nina and where he dumped the body. In exchange, Reiser will be sentenced to 15 years to life for a reduced charge of second-degree murder. On July 7, 2008, Reiser took the authorities to Redwood Regional Park, near Oakland Hills, California, where he buried Nina. This is one of those unusual cases where a plea agreement was still agreed after a full jury trial. This case clearly justifies the need to abolish plea bargaining. Most of the proponents of plea bargaining argue that plea bargaining saves taxpayers the costs of a jury trial. But here is a case where after a prolonged jury trial, a plea bargain was still offered by the prosecutor. Is this what is meant by saving the costs of trial? Plea bargaining is a ridiculous practice that serves the best interest of a guilty offender. Here is a situation where the jury verdict was superseded by a plea bargain by a prosecutor. It is worrying that contemporary societies do not see anything wrong with this kind of practice. This is a case of a cold-blooded killer who struck his wife in the head, then strangled her to death, put the body into a duffel bag and then dumped the body into a shallow grave in the woods. This case clearly exemplifies the evils of plea bargaining. Here is a killer who was offered the opportunity by the prosecutor to even use his wife's body as a plea bargaining 'item.' Plea bargaining is clearly in the best interests of a guilty offender. Should we continue to give sentence discounts to guilty and in most cases very dangerous offenders?

1.7 VICTIM PARTICIPATION IN PLEA BARGAINING

The issue of whether victims should be given the right to participate in plea bargaining is another major concern that has been addressed by some associations and scholars. In fact, The American Bar Association in its Standards for Criminal Justice, Pleas of Guilty, stated that "The prosecuting attorney should make every effort to remain advised of the attitudes and sentiments of victims and law enforcement officials before reaching a plea agreement."[174] Sarah Welling maintained that victims should be accorded the right to participate in plea bargains, but within certain limits.[175] She believes that victims should be given the right to be informed of the terms of the bargain; the date, time, and place of the hearing; the right to be present at the hearing where the bargain will be presented to the court; and the right to participate in the plea bargaining decision.[176] Some scholars are, however, critical of victim participation in plea bargaining. It has been noted that the problems with victim participation in plea bargaining include: (1) hindering the prosecutor aim of quick disposition of cases, (2) leading to the plea bargaining process becoming confrontational, and (3) "victim participation might render plea bargains more risky for and therefore less attractive to defendants."[177] In response to these concerns about victim participation in plea bargains, Welling maintained that:

> Victim participation may increase the risk to the defendant that the judge will reject the bargain, but resolution of the case will still be fast and certain if plea bargain is accepted. Thus plea bargains may be more risky to the defendant as a result of victim participation, but they will still retain other attractive qualities. At any rate, in one study the empirical evidence indicated that victim participation did not decrease the number of plea bargains entered and did not disrupt speedy disposition. Second, the evidence conflicts on whether reducing plea bargaining creates a corresponding decrease in the number of guilty pleas. Third, as a policy matter, the need of administrative efficiency should not determine the structure of our criminal justice system. Rather, the search for justice should determine the system's structure.[178]

Victim participation in plea bargains would advance various interests of the victim and society without any significant detrimental impact to the interests of prosecutors and defendants.[179] Welling further maintained that victim participation should be limited in two ways as follows:

> First, this participation right is only a right to be heard by the trial court; the victim would have no right to appeal and challenge the trial court's decision on acceptance of the plea bargain. Second, the right would also be limited in that if the trial judge denied the victim the right to be heard, no cause of action would be generated for the victim. Instead, the victim would have the option of filing a complaint against the judge with the appropriate judicial review commission. Within these limits, victims would have a right to participate but would not be able to control the plea bargain; nor would the existence of this right generate additional litigation to burden the system.[180]

Welling concluded that victims should be accorded the right to be heard by the trial judge before the plea bargain is accepted.[181] She noted that three states already have this kind of practice, but observed that the consultation rights in these states are flawed.[182]

1.8 CONCLUSION

Plea bargaining is a process that does not safeguard an innocent defendant. Plea bargaining has poisoned the criminal justice system to the extent that asking for a trial has become a crime and you get punished severely for it. This is the aftermath of plea bargaining and therein lies one of the justifications for its abolition. Plea bargaining operates by threats and nothing but the threats.

Plea bargaining is in the best interest of a guilty defendant. Under plea bargaining, a guilty defendant gets a lesser sentence, gets some charges dismissed, avoids going through the rigors of a trial, avoids a pre-trial detention, gets the case disposed of quickly, avoids the deterrent effect of publicity, and gets a less serious offense entered in his or her criminal record. Society as a whole loses because offenders do not get the appropriate punishment. As a result, guilty and often dangerous offenders are being rushed in and out of the system. They get lesser sentences and then get sent back to the community to commit further crimes. In the end, society loses in this "game."

If there is no plea bargaining, then many of the innocent defendants will not be charged for crimes that they did not commit, as prosecutors have to gather sufficient evidence before they could bring up charges. The advocates of plea bargaining continue to look at the process purely in economic terms. Yes, plea bargaining saves time and money, but in the long run justice is not seen to be served. Money and the Due Process should not be interdependent.

It is submitted that plea bargaining re-victimizes. Victims, more often than not, would want to see the offenders punished fully according to the law. But, under plea bargaining, offenders do not get the adequate or maximum punishment. Thus, victims are being re-victimized by the plea bargaining process.

This book therefore calls for the abolition of plea bargaining. There is an alternative to plea bargaining and that is trial by a judge, which has been proven to be efficient and not as expensive as advocates of plea bargaining fear. Professor Schulhofer's study of Philadelphia's trial system has shown that trial by a judge has worked for many decades, and actually cuts down the cost of giving every defendant a jury trial. "This system has worked in practice very effectively for many, many years, so it's not an imaginary idea, and it essentially solves 99 or 100 percent of the problems we've been discussing."[183] A study by Professor Alschuler also showed that:

> ...the United States could provide three-day jury trials to all felony defendants, who reach the trial stage by adding no more than an estimated $850 million to annual criminal justice expenditures. Moreover, it contends that the actual cost of implementing a plea

> bargaining prohibition would be less than this amount, in part because most cases now resolved through plea bargaining could be tried in less than three days and, even more importantly, because many defendants would plead guilty without bargaining.[184]

CHAPTER 2
PSYCHIC INVESTIGATION OF CRIME

2.1 INTRODUCTION

There is a great deal of skepticism surrounding the use of psychics in crime investigations. Is this because many people do not understand the foundation of this method, or is it because many people believe that this area falls into the "unknown" and should remain there? It is against this background that I have decided to write on this topic and try to find the true position. Is there a scientific basis to psychic abilities? Does this method satisfy the general acceptance standard or the *Daubert* standard required for the legal admissibility of new scientific techniques? Should psychics be used in crime investigations? These questions and many more have been examined. Examples of cases where psychics contributed to crime-solving have also been examined. It should be noted that when psychics are called to assist in crime investigations, they are specifically asked to provide information with particular reference to the person or the case being investigated. They do not perform personality evaluations. In the conclusion section, I have examined what the future holds for the use of psychics in crime investigations. This book supports the use of psychics in crime investigations. However, this book concludes that psychics should not be allowed to testify in courts.

2.2 WHO IS A PSYCHIC?

A psychic is any person who can receive thoughts and impressions telepathically, can see events extrasensorily, and can gather information about an object by holding that object without using the normal five senses.[185] Arguably, the idea of using psychics in crime investigations falls under the discipline of parapsychology. Parapsychology refers to the scientific study of extrasensory perception (ESP), mind-matter interaction, and survival, which are unusual events associated with human experience.[186] There is common belief that psychic or paranormal abilities are not scientific. Hence, parapsychology is usually referred to as pseudoscience. As Susan Blackmore has pointed out:

> Parapsychology has been a controversial science since its inception, with experimenters claiming results that cannot be explained by chance, and critics arguing that the best explanations are methodological flaws, statistical errors, or outright fraud. Methods have gradually improved, but the goal of a conclusively convincing demonstration or a repeatable experiment has not been achieved. Fully automated experiments have provided new evidence, and meta-analyses have revealed consistent features in whole areas of research.[187]

It should be noted that it is not only psychics who face fraudulent accusation. There is fraud also in other practices, including medicine. There is common belief that people are born with psychic abilities. However, some people can develop psychic or intuitive abilities later in life. Psychics work from their home offices and also visit crime scenes. Psychics normally request items belonging to the victim or the missing person. By touching these items, psychics believe that they can communicate with the person's spirit and get information about the person and what happened. Psychics also usually request a photograph of the missing persons or victims. There is no specific educational requirement needed to be a psychic, which creates a dilemma when psychic investigation is classified under the discipline of parapsychology. They are not usually academically trained psychologists.

Psychic abilities are all about extra-sensory perception. And extrasensory perception is "the reception of information by means other than the usual physical senses and without using logical inference. ESP (also referred to as psi) is a blanket term covering most psychic abilities but is generally divided into the specific abilities of telepathy, clairvoyance, and precognition."[188] The different types of psychic abilities include the following:

Clairvoyance: Clairvoyance is a type of extrasensory perception whereby psychics can remotely obtain information about places or events that cannot usually be obtained by the normal senses. There are two forms of clairvoyance. The first is clairaudience, which refers to the ability to obtain extrasensory information through sounds; and the second is clairsentience, which is the ability to obtain extrasensory information through feeling.[189]

Dowsing: Dowsing refers to the type of extrasensory perception usually used in finding missing persons. With dowsing, "underground water, minerals objects (e.g., bodies, artifacts, lost articles) are located by sensitive individuals, usually with the aid of a dowsing rod or pendulum. A specific form of dowsing involves the use of maps and aerial photos in place of working on-site."[190]

Precognition: Precognition refers to the ability to obtain information about future occurrences and events. It is different from premonition, which is the ability that enables psychics to warn people about something that will happen to them in the future.[191]

Psychokinesis (PK): Psychokinesis, also known as mind-matter interaction, is a form of extrasensory perception whereby the mind can influence objects, time, matter, and space. Psychokinesis may be divided into two kinds.[192] The first is micro-PK "which is usually inferred from the nonrandom behavior of random event generators (REGs)."[193] The second kind is macro-PK which is observed directly.[194] The micro-PK can be internal or external, and "internal micro-PK may underlie voluntary behavior within the body, while external micro-PK appears as voluntary behavior that occurs outside the body."[195]

Psychometry: This is the form of extrasensory perception whereby an object can be used to gather/reveal past experiences or past events related to that object. It should be noted that psychometry is sometimes seen as a type retrocognition.[196] Retrocognition is the extrasensory perception ability to experience and have knowledge of past events which cannot be obtained by the normal senses.[197]

Remote Viewing: Remote viewing (RV) involves using psychic ability to describe remote places, events or objects.

> Remote viewers often can contact, experience, and describe a hidden object or a remote natural or architectural site based on the presence of a cooperative person at the location, geographical coordinates, or some other target demarcation, which we call an address. Shape, form, and color are described much more reliably than the target's functions or other analytical information. In addition to this vivid visual imagery, viewers sometimes describe associated feelings, sounds, smells, and even electrical or magnetic fields. Blueprint accuracy sometimes can be achieved, and reliability in a series can be as high as 70%. With practice, people become increasingly able to separate out the psychic signal from the mental noise of memory, analysis, and imagination. Targets and target details as small as 1mm can be perceived.[198]

Research has shown that distance is not a problem in remote viewing.[199] It has also been noted that remote viewing is "a natural and widely distributed ability for which everyone, to a greater or lesser degree, has the potential."[200] Remote viewing experiments were carried out at the Stanford Research Institute (SRI) from 1972 to 1986.[201] Russell Targ and Hal Puthoff, both physicists, were two of the remote viewing experimenters at the SRI. According to Targ, one of the assignments they were given at SRI was "to describe a Soviet research and development laboratory at a particular latitude and longitude in the

USSR. The psychic description that we and our viewer provided to our sponsor was so outstanding that it alone assured our funding for the next several years."[202]

Patrick H. Price, former police commissioner of Burbank, California, is one of the most famous remote viewers. He was involved with most of the remote reviewing experiments at the Stanford Research Institute. He has been described as "a psychic treasure."[203] There were reports that "he would sit with the despatcher in the police station, and whenever he heard a crime reported, he would psychically scan the city and send a car to the spot where he saw a frightened man hiding."[204]

Major General Albert Stubblebine, former head of The United States Army's Intelligence and Security Command (INSCOM), was reported to have used psychics in remote-viewing the house of General Manuel Noriega, former military leader of Panama. In an operation called "Landbroker" the psychics were asked to provide detailed information about Noriega's house, and "the result was a two-page top-secret report laying out the rooms and their contents. Unfortunately, once again, the operation was aborted before agents could get into the house to confirm the findings."[205]

Telepathy: Telepathy is a form of psychic ability whereby information is transferred directly from one person's mind to another. It involves direct intuitive experience of somebody else's thoughts and mental state. Telepathy is used by psychics to obtain information about an offender's motives, state of mind, and the veracity of the offender's statements.[206] It is also used to communicate with the spirits of deceased victims.[207]

In the words of Hibbard, Worring, and Brennan, "all the above abilities have been tested scientifically, and some of the results have been astounding. When laboratory evidence is lacking (which is sometimes the case because some psychic abilities and phenomena cannot be generated on demand), there is a wealth of anecdotal and well-documented experiences by credible persons."[208]

2.3 HISTORICAL OVERVIEW

The idea of using psychics in crime investigations could be traced back to the biblical time when in the first book of Samuel, chapter 9, Kish sent out his son Saul and his servants to go and look for his lost asses, and after three days without any luck, they went to consult a local seer named Samuel, who told them to go back home because the lost asses will return after three days.[209] Michel de Nostredame (1503-1566), known as Nostradamus, is considered one of the greatest psychics of all times. He was a French apothecary and seer known for his ability to predict world events. However, the first psychic to assist in crime investigation, *per se,* is Jacques Aymar, a French man. It was reported that on July 5, 1692, in the city of Lyons, a wine merchant and his wife were brutally hacked to death with a butcher's cleaver during a robbery. Aymar, from Saint Marcellin, Province of Dauphine, who used a divining rod in his psychic practice, was asked by the King's procurator to assist in the investigation into the murders, and it was reported that he helped find the murderer.[210]

Psychics continued to operate widely and freely in many European countries until 1810 when there was a need to protect some citizens from some fraudulent fortune-tellers. Hence, in 1810, the French Legislature added a provision to their Penal Code, prohibiting the practice of fortune-telling.[211] Kate and Margaret Fox, known as the Fox Sisters, were notable spiritualists around 1847 and they claimed to hear spirits rapping in their home in Hydesville, New York. In the 1860s Charles Forster, a medium, from Salem in Massachusetts was reported to have assisted in the investigation of crimes. In 1863, German states followed the footsteps of the French legislature and decided to protect individuals from fraudulent fortune-tellers, clairvoyants, and spiritualists. The kingdom of Bavaria, for instance, added a clause in their Penal Code stating that "He who, in return for a fee or for gaining any other benefit, engages in the performance of so-called witchcraft or exorcism, fortune-telling, card-reading, treasure-seeking, explanation of omens or dreams, or other similar magic practices, shall be liable to confinement for a term not exceeding fourteen days or to the imposition of a fine."[212]

In 1882 the British Society for Psychical Research was formed in London. This was followed by the formation of the American Society for Psychical Research in 1885. In the United Kingdom, the Fraudulent Mediums Act of 1951 repealed the Witchcraft Act of 1735. The Fraudulent Mediums Act of 1951 made it an offense for any individual to receive money or other valuable things as a reward by claiming to be psychics, mediums, or spiritualists. This Act was, however, repealed on May 26, 2008 when the Consumer Protection from Unfair Trading Regulations 2008 came into effect.

In 1922, Eugenie Dennis, from Atchison, Kansas, became widely recognized as a psychic who was very successful in finding missing persons and items. Dennis helped the police recover fifteen stolen bicycles in Joplin, Missouri; provided vital information to the police, which led to the recovery of twenty-three stolen diamonds in Omaha, Nebraska, and it was reported that she received more than 800,000 letters from people asking her for help.[213]

In the 1930s Janos Kele, a Hungarian clairvoyant, was reported to be 80 percent accurate in his predictions. In fact, Kele's psychic abilities were examined by Professor Hans Driesch and his colleagues at Leipzig University and they concluded that Kele was an "extraordinary psychic" and "classic clairvoyant."[214] Dr. Karlis Osis, of Duke University's parapsychology laboratory, also examined Kele's psychic/diagnostic abilities and concluded that Kele was accurate in the psychic analysis.[215] It was reported that Kele helped locate a Hungarian refugee missing in Argentina.

In 1934, Dr. J. B. Rhine, of Duke University Parapsychology Laboratory, came up with Extra-Sensory

Perception (ESP). The four areas of ESP are telepathy, which involves direct mind-to-mind communication; clairvoyance, which means knowing about something elsewhere in space; precognition, which means knowing about the future, and psychokinesis (PK), which means a direct influence of the mind upon matter.[216] Another notable psychic is Peter Hurkos, a Dutch psychic who in 1941 assisted the police in many cases, through his clairvoyancy. Vanga Dimitrova, a Hungarian clairvoyant, was studied by Dr. Lozanov and a government appointed board of examiners, and they rated her highly and concluded that she was genuine, and the state decided to employ her in 1966.[217] Beverly Jaegars, from Sappington, Missouri, a remote viewer, is also another notable psychic who was reported to have assisted the police. She founded a remote viewing agency called U.S. PSI Squad in 1971.

Philip Jordan, a deputy sheriff at Tioga Sheriff's Office, New York assisted the police in many states in the United States. In fact, James Coons of the Vermont Sheriff's Office (Addison County), spoke highly of Jordan and maintained that Jordan "located a lot of missing persons. His big thing is bodies. He has a documented track record that's very credible. We might be able to use him as a contributing factor to probable cause as a basis for a search warrant."[218] Any discussion of psychics, especially in the United States will be incomplete without mentioning Noreen Reiner. In 1981, she presented lectures at the FBI Academy, at Quantico, Virginia. It was reported that she foresaw the assassination attempt on President Ronald Reagan some months before the assassination attempt. Other notable psychics include Sylvia Brown, Carla Baron, Char Margolis, John Anderson, John Edwards, Annette Martin, James Van Praagh, Allison DuBois, Robert Brown, Valerie Morrison, Patrick Burns, John Oliver, and Rose Kopp.

It has been noted that the growing interest in psychics may be because many high profile individuals have consulted psychics, and also because of the ever increasing television shows on psychics. Notable individuals who have consulted astrologers, psychics, and spiritual healers include Nancy Reagan, wife of former President Ronald Reagan, Diana, Princess of Wales, and former England football manager, Glen Hoddle.[219]

Despite its long history, the use of psychics in crime investigations is still viewed with great skepticism. Several reasons account for this situation. In fact, it has been observed that (1) the police and the members of the public who have used psychics "may be reluctant to reveal information to outsiders due to embarrassment, fear of publicity, or other personal motivations," (2) psychics may bc cxaggerating their success because they want to "enhance their reputations, self-esteem and incomes," and (3) the media may be reporting psychic success stories without checking their accuracy.[220]

2.4 IS THERE A SCIENTIFIC BASIS TO PSYCHIC ABILITIES?

Even though a lot of research work has been carried out on this topic, there is still no general agreement in the scientific community on the scientific basis of psychic abilities. But it is commonly acknowledged that there are certain phenomena that cannot be explained under the normal senses and circumstances. Therefore, it is submitted that there is some truth about psychic abilities. The problem of lack of agreement on the scientific basis of psychic abilities has been clearly outlined by Luis A. Cordon. He states:

> The essential problem is that a large portion of the scientific community, including most research psychologists, regard parapsychology as a pseudoscience, due largely to its failure to move beyond null results in the way science does. Ordinarily, when experimental evidence fails repeatedly to support a hypothesis, that hypothesis is abandoned. Within parapsychology, however, more than a century of experimentation has failed even to conclusively demonstrate the mere existence of paranormal phenomena, yet parapsychologists continue to pursue that elusive goal.[221]

As Allan Combs has pointed out, it seems that "critics of psi research force it to meet a standard to which ordinary research itself patently fails to measure."[222]Are there neurobiological explanations of psi abilities? Some studies point to a relationship between brain waves and the mental states associated with psi abilities. It should be noted that:

> The brain generates streams of electric activity from its surface that can be detected by an electroencephalograph (EEG). There are five types of brain waves, distinguished by their association with different mental states and frequency in cycles per second, or hertz (Hz): gamma waves (30-80 Hz) appear when we process complex sensory information; beta waves (13-29 Hz) appear when we are alert and attentive; alpha waves (8-12 Hz) appear when we are relaxed and disengaged from thought as in mediations; theta waves (3.5-7.5 Hz) often appear in deeper mediative states, but more commonly when we are drowsy and falling asleep; and delta waves appear during deep sleep and have the slowest wave cycles (Cahn and Polish, 2006). We produce all five types in the course of a 24-hour day and, at the end of days, 0 Hz, the sign of death.[223]

After reviewing several psi studies involving brain waves, William G. Roll and Bryan J. Williams found a positive relationship between alpha and telepathy/clairvoyance in six studies; found a negative relationship between alpha and precognition in one study, and concluded that "a state of relaxed attention may be conducive to telepathy and clairvoyance."[224]

Roll and Williams in their examination of the issue of whether alpha feedback is positively or negatively related to extrasensory perception, found evidence suggesting the existence of both positive and negative relationships. They noted as follows:

> A study by Lewis and Schmeidler (1971) suggests both. Initially, they found a positive relationship when their participants did not know that they were engaging in an ESP test (the test was covertly embedded in their training), and then found a negative relationship when participants knew they were being tested for ESP. A possible solution to this quandary comes from Rao and Feola's (1973) ESP test of a male participant who had previously received extensive alpha training. The participant showed higher ESP scores when asked to produce alpha than when asked to suppress alpha. The solution then may be to limit this type of research to participants already proficient in manipulating their alpha. Another study, by Venturino (1978), found no relationship between alpha training and ESP, but the study also showed no evidence for ESP and is therefore inconclusive.
>
> In summary, two alpha training studies showed a positive relationship between alpha and ESP, a third showed a negative relationship, a fourth showed both, and a fifth was inconclusive. In short, it is unknown whether or not alpha feedback enhances ESP.[225]

An ESP-Alpha connection can also be determined by examining whether there are changes in the frequency of alpha waves during ESP tests.[226] Some studies found that "increases in alpha frequency, from the time participants began to relax to the time they reported their impression of the ESP target, were associated with higher ESP scores." (Stanford, 1971; Stanford and Lovin, 1970; Stanford and Stanford, 1969; Stanford and Stevenson, 1972.)[227] The increased arousal and attentiveness required to make extrasensory perception responses could be the reason why there was an increase in the alpha frequency.[228]

An ESP-Alpha connection may also be determined by examining the changes in the amplitude.[229] By amplitude, we mean "the strength of alpha waves as shown by their height on the EEG record during an ESP test."[230] This method has been used to monitor the EEG of a female psychic claimant during remote viewing and also used to examine changes in amplitude while recording the EEG of three remote viewers.[231] The EEG of the research participants did not show any associated amplitude but the participants produced evidence for ESP.[232]

Functional magnetic resonance imaging and ESP

Functional magnetic resonance imaging (fMRI) is another method for monitoring brain activity. The difference between fMRI and common magnetic resonance image (cMRI) is that fMRI "provides ongoing impressions of neural activity," while cMRI is static.[233] Roll and Williams examined five fMRI studies of ESP and one study "suggests the visual cortex may reflect presentiment responses." Two of the studies expanded on brain correlations between bonded pairs and "both revealed changes in a receiver's visual cortex when a sender was stimulated but, strangely enough, one study found reduced cortical activity while the other found increased activity."[234] The other two studies were omitted because of shortcomings.[235] Roll and Williams concluded that "studies with both normal and psychic claimants suggest psi is associated with well-known neurobiological processes, especially with brain waves in the alpha and theta range. On the other hand, there is little if any evidence that ESP is facilitated by alpha feedback, frequency, or amplitude."[236]

Is precognition a normal brain function? Some studies suggest that precognition may actually be a normal brain function that involves brain voltage. In fact, Roll and Williams carried out studies involving individuals who claimed that they did not possess psychic abilities and found that;

> precognition (including presentience) may be associated with brain voltage as shown by ERP, SCP, and CNV. Because ERP, SCP, and CNV

> reflect normal brain functions, their seeming association with precognitive occurrences indicates that precognition may likewise be a normal brain function. There are indications that ESP may be associated with the right brain hemisphere of ordinary people, but there is little if any experimental confirmation of this. Frequent ESP experiences among the general population may also be associated with increased temporal lobe sensitivity.[237]

There is evidence indicating that higher activities occur in the frontal and prefrontal cortex during religious experiences.[238]Hence, it has been argued that "mediumistic and trance experiences as well as intense mystical, religious, and spiritual experiences are distinct and mediated by several brain regions and systems."[239] It has been recognized that "increased activity in the frontal cortex may reflect focused concentration during the altered states of consciousness (ASC) experiences elicited by meditation practices, while the correlation between the dorsolateral prefrontal cortex and the superior parietal lobe may reflect a nonordinary sense of space and time."[240]

At this point it should be noted that the Central Intelligence Agency (CIA) sponsored a program that investigated ESP and its potential as a law enforcement tool. The CIA, in June 1995 conducted a retrospective review of the STARGATE research program, including an analysis of anomalous cognition, and concluded among other things that "a statistically significant laboratory effect has been demonstrated, but more replications were needed."[241] The validity of the conclusions made by the CIA was, however, questioned by some scholars. Edwin May, for instance, questioned the validity of the conclusions, arguing that the CIA/AIR:

> Limited the data sets in the analysis. As a way of officially ignoring anomalous cognition's positive contributions to intelligence, only a small fraction of the operational remote viewing database was examined. That was the final data

collected just before the unit closed, a time widely known as problematic. In their laboratory evaluations, they restricted the investigation to only the government-sponsored research and then insisted on the need for more outside replications. In doing so, they ignored the conclusions of one of their own investigators who showed that the government-sponsored research had already been conceptually replicated.

Failed to contact significant program participants. Because of the complexity of the 24-year program, it is impossible to conduct an in-depth and accurate evaluation without significant contact with the program's many major participants. The project's reports were written to satisfy specific contract requirements and were not designed individually or in total to serve as a program justification; thus, these documents provide a substantially incomplete picture of the program.[242]

May found errors with the evaluation methodology, and maintained that he has "become reluctantly convinced that their conclusions were set before their investigations began."[243] May contended that the investigators failed to do the following:

Apply consistent criteria for acceptance or rejection of anomalous cognition. The investigators were troubled by possible non-AC alternative explanations for the statistically significant laboratory results, yet ignored similar alternatives for the failed operations. For example, well-known psychological effects such as bad morale, failed expectations, and a lack of a supportive environment, were not discussed as potential alternatives for the operations. In their positive forms, all of these psychological effects are critical for excellence in any human activity.

Avail themselves of the previous exhaustive reviews conducted by various organizations within the DOD, all but one of which was positive. Since the CIA was allowed only four months to complete the evaluation, it is surprising that they chose not to use this resource.

Reject a discredited evaluation of parapsychology conducted by the National Research Council (NRC). They knew that the NRC investigators were not cleared for the vast majority of SRI's research, yet the AIR investigations relied heavily on the NRC's review to question the SRI research results prior to 1988.

Use neutral government scientific evaluation resources such as the Military Services' or the CIA's Scientific Advisory Boards. Instead they commissioned external investigators with previously published conclusions about parapsychology. The CIA could then justify whatever conclusions they wished, because it would be consistent, by definition, with at least one of their external reviewers.

To recognize a potential significant conflict of interest for Dr. David Goslin, president of AIR and a report co-author. He had administrative responsibility for the discredited NRC investigation of parapsychology.[244]

May was highly critical of the review and he wrote, "Aside from setting the record straight, I felt obligated to show that as the result of their seriously flawed methodology, the CIA/AIR greatly underestimated the statistical robustness of the research results and significantly undervalued the potential for anomalous cognition in intelligence operations."[245]

2.5 PSYCHICS AND CRIME INVESTIGATION

Despite the general skepticism about psychics, they have assisted the police in crime investigations in many cases, especially in the United States and Canada. There is evidence to suggest that the police in many states in the United States use psychics.[246] It has been noted that it is usually the psychics who contact the police or sheriff's office offering information about a crime.[247] Sometimes, family members also contact the psychics themselves or they may request the police to bring in a psychic to help speed up the investigation. The question becomes—how do psychics assist in crime investigations?

Psychics assist the police in finding dead bodies, missing persons, lost pets, lost items, and also help in finding those responsible for a crime. They can provide crucial information about the location of an attack, weapons used, and the place where the suspect may be found. Psychics can also recreate crime scenes, detailing events leading to the crime, during the crime, and after the crime. In 1983, Greta Alexander, an American psychic assisted the police in a murder case in Illinois. Detective William Fitzgerald was in charge of this case. In this murder case, the victim, Mary L. Cousett, from Alton in Illinois left her home on April 24, 1983 with her boyfriend, Stanley Holiday, Jr., and did not return home. Her body was not found, but police investigations pointed to Holiday being the killer. He was arrested and charged with the murder. The police had no witnesses and with the body not found, they decided to ask Greta Alexander for help. It was reported that Alexander provided the police with information about the location of the body and also gave vital distinctive information about the killer.[248]

According to Detective Fitzgerald, 22 things that Alexander said relating to the crime turned out to be correct, including (1) that the head and a foot would be separated from the body, (2) the letter *S* will be significant, and (3) the man who found the body will have a "bad hand."[249] It was reported that when the body was found, the skull was separated from the body, the left foot was missing and the auxiliary policeman, Steve Trew, who found the body had a deformed left hand, as Alexander had told them.[250]

Another case worth mentioning is the murder case of Etheridge in Lompoc, California in 1978, when psychic Dixie Yeterian assisted the police. After handling Etheridge's wrist watch and ring, Yeterian "saw" that Etheridge had been shot dead by his own son—Owen Etheridge, who actually contacted her for help. Etheridge was questioned about his father's death, and after he was informed of the psychic's information that he was involved in the murder, he confessed to having committed the murder.[251]

Psychics also assist police artists by providing physical descriptions of suspects they claim are responsible for crimes. They can provide information relating to the race, height, body build, items, and the type of weapon the suspect used during the attack. In some cases, attorneys have hired psychics to assist them in jury selections. This is one of the most controversial issues in the use of psychics. At this point, it should be noted that psychics tend to achieve best results when dealing with cases involving strong emotions, such as murder. It has been observed that, "Emotions such as terror, hate, fear, create lingering vibrations, they say, that are picked up by the psychic, who acts as an antenna."[252]

From the above discussion, one question that arises is the question of whether psychics should be used in crime investigations. Scholars differ on this issue. Research by Lyons and Truzzi found evidence for and against the use of psychics in crime investigations.[253] They pointed out the problem of proof in psychic practice, but concluded that "nonproof does not constitute disproof."[254] Lyons and Truzzi further concluded that "the existing data—large as we have shown them to be—simply remain inadequate for us to reach rational judgment that is simply pro or con. It remains wise to doubt the blue sense, but it is scientific folly to deny it categorically."[255] They noted however, that the validity of psi cannot be proved beyond a reasonable doubt.[256]

In their own examination of the use of psychics in crime investigations, Hibbard, Worring and Brennan maintained that psychics should be used in crime investigations when they wrote, "Let us hope that those in authority in the United States have the foresight and open-mindedness to seriously consider and explore the use of psychics in criminology."[257] They called for the introduction of guidelines for the use of psychics by police departments. On the future of using psychics in crime investigations, they maintained that:

> In decades to come, psychic criminology likely will chart a common course, known as the 'boom and bust' cycle. The first stage of the cycle is one of open skepticism and criticism, but with time and exposure the skeptics and critics realize the value of the new idea and become proponents — the second stage. The new proponents overenthusiastically embrace the technique - the third stage. When it fails to meet their unrealistically high expectations, however, they abandon it - the fourth stage. Hopefully, when psychic criminology is first widely embraced, it will be accepted and used professionally and in moderation. If unrealistic expectations are withheld and it is developed and used properly, it will take a legitimate place in the investigator's armamentarium.[258]

Hibbard, Worring, and Brennan also maintained that there will be a surge in the use of psychics in crime investigations in the future. For them, scientific corroboration will lead to this surge. They gave the example of graphology and hypnosis, which "were once considered superstitious nonsense, both are now accepted as valid scientific tools and are used by law enforcement as investigative tools. We believe the same holds true for psychic abilities."[259] Hugo Meynell also supports the idea of using psychics in the investigation of crime. He maintained that "the case for the reality of a large proportion of the classes of events usually termed paranormal is very strong; and that some of these, in spite of the popularity of the counterarguments, provide substantial grounds for belief in life after death for human beings."[260]

Some scholars, however, are critical of the use of psychics in crime investigations. Some have noted the issue of cognitive biases[261] and the Barnum effect. The Barnum effect refers to the idea that most people will believe that general personality statements or descriptions apply to them specifically, even though those statements are in fact general and could apply to many people. Alison, Smith, and Morgan carried out two studies in order to test the hypothesis that individuals will perceive ambiguous statements as being relatively accurate descriptions of strangers when the statements are presented to them as offender profiles.[262] Their study involved 46 police officers from a police force in The United Kingdom, who they grouped into two. The first group was given a genuine offender description, while the second group was given a fake one. The first group was made up of 19 males and three females, while the second group was made up of 15 males and nine females. Based on the two studies, Alison et al. believed and concluded that "individuals are prepared to perceive ambiguous statements, when presented in the form of an offender profile, as being relatively accurate descriptions of complete strangers."[263]

However, a study by MacDonald & Standing in 2002 indicated that self-serving bias is powerful enough to cancel the Barnum effect. They carried out a study involving 27 undergraduate psychology students with the aim of ascertaining "whether or not people will accept positive statements, but reject negative statements about themselves, so as to test for a relationship between the Barnum effect and the phenomenon of self-serving bias"[264] The study produced very interesting results. According to this study, gender and demand characteristics showed no significant effect, and "it appears that the self-serving bias is powerful enough to cancel the usual Barnum effect, in which subjects typically show marked gullibility for statements about themselves."[265]

The use of psychics in crime investigations should be differentiated from their involvement in tarot readings and horoscopes. When psychics are called to assist in crime investigations, they are specifically asked to provide information with particular reference to the person or the case being investigated. They do not provide general statements or general descriptions. There are usually no question and answer sessions. Therefore, the Barnum effect, arguably, does not apply when discussing the use of psychics in crime investigations. When assisting in crime investigations, psychics provide specific information based specifically on the person, and this most times involves holding objects owned by that person.

2.6 LEGAL ASPECTS OF USING PSYCHICS

Courts in almost all jurisdictions have always battled with the decision to admit or exclude novel scientific techniques. Hence, when new techniques or methods are developed, courts have to ensure the reliability and validity of such techniques or methods before they can be admitted as evidence. In fact, Professor Andre Moenssens maintained that "where a person's freedom is at stake, courts ought to be more reluctant to admit evidence based on new, as yet unproven, techniques when such evidence is being offered by the prosecution."[266] In the United States, this problem is compounded by the fact that there are three main rules/standards governing the admissibility of scientific evidence. The first is the *Frye* standard also known as the General Acceptance Rule. *Frye* is a 1923 decision by the United States Court of Appeals for the District of Columbia, in a case where the admissibility of opinion derived from a systolic blood pressure deception test (this is the early form of polygraph lie detector test) was challenged. In *Frye v. United States*,[267] The Court of Appeals ruled that scientific evidence is admissible if the methods and principles underlying it had achieved widespread acceptance in the relevant discipline.

Delivering the decision of the Court, Justice Van Orsdel stated that:

> Just when a scientific principle or discovery crosses the line between the experimental and demonstrable stages is difficult to define. Somewhere in this twilight zone the evidential force of the principle must be recognized, and while courts will go a long way in admitting expert testimony deduced from a well-recognized scientific principle or discovery, the thing from which the deduction is made must be sufficiently established to have gained general acceptance in the particular field in which it belongs.[268]

Even though the *Frye* decision faced a lot of criticisms, it still remained one of the main rules governing the admissibility of expert testimony in the United States. The second rule governing the admissibility of scientific evidence is the *Federal Rules of Evidence,*[269] rule 702, adopted in 1975. Rule 702 states the following:

> If scientific, technical or other specialized knowledge will assist the trier of fact to understand the evidence or to determine a fact in issue, a witness qualified as an expert by knowledge, skill, experience, training, or education may testify thereto in the form of an opinion or otherwise, if (1) the testimony is based upon sufficient facts or data, (2) the testimony is the product of reliable principles and methods, and (3) the witness has applied the principles and methods reliably to the facts of the case.[270]

The Federal Rules of Evidence lays emphasis on the relevance and reliability of a principle, method or technique. The Rule also stresses that the testimony should assist judges and jurors in understanding the facts of the case.

The United States Supreme Court decision in *Daubert v. Merrell Dow Pharmaceuticals* is the third rule governing the admissibility of scientific evidence in the United States. In this case, the United States Supreme Court, through Justice Harry Blackmun stated that when:

> Faced with a proffer of expert scientific testimony under Rule 702, the trial judge pursuant to Rule 104(a), must make a preliminary assessment of whether the testimony's underlying reasoning or methodology is scientifically valid and properly can be applied to the facts at issue. Many considerations will bear on the inquiry, including whether the theory or technique in question can be (and has been) tested, whether it has been subjected to peer review and publication, its known or potential error rate and the existence and maintenance of standards controlling its operation, and whether it has attracted widespread acceptance within a relevant scientific community. The inquiry is a flexible one, and its focus must be solely on principles and methodology, not on conclusions that they generate. Throughout, the judge should also be mindful of other applicable Rules.[271]

The Supreme Court also stated that trial judges have the function to act as "gatekeepers" and determine whether the testimony is reliable and scientifically valid. In a nutshell, *Daubert* emphasizes the relevance, reliability, and validity of any principle, method, or technique, and also requires trial judges to look at four key factors—testability, peer review, error rate, and general acceptance—when faced with the decision of whether to admit or exclude any expert testimony.

Expert testimony by psychics is generally inadmissible. Under both *Frye* and *Daubert,* admitting expert testimony by a psychic as evidence appears to be problematic at the moment. The method of using psychics in crime investigation is not generally accepted. The method has not been shown by current research studies to be reliable as to be used as evidence. The scientific basis of psychic abilities has not been adequately demonstrated. It should be noted, however, that a technique or method does not have to be scientific for it to be admitted as evidence. Under a strict *Daubert* standard, it has to be demonstrated that a method or technique can be tested or has been tested, has been peer-reviewed, been subjected to publication, reliable, and has achieved widespread acceptance in the relevant discipline. The *Federal Rule of Evidence 702* and *Daubert* also require that the testimony be based upon sufficient facts or data. As it stands, the use of psychics in crime investigations, based on psychic abilities, does not satisfy a strict application of *Frye* and *Daubert.* However, in the case of Susan Polk[272] in California, a psychic was allowed to testify in court. The psychic should not have been allowed to testify. It is noteworthy to point out that the *Frye* standard seems to be more liberal than *Daubert.* The State of California uses the *Frye* standard.

Susan Polk (Susan Mae Bolling) was charged with first-degree murder of her husband Dr. Felix Polk, a psychotherapist, in 2002. She was accused of stabbing her husband to death on October 13, 2002 at their $2 million home in Orinda, California. She was his patient when she was 15 years old, and they later got married. Daniel Horowitz was representing Susan, but following the killing of his wife, Pamela Vitale, he could not continue as Susan's attorney. Susan represented herself after firing her attorneys. At the trial that took place at Contra Costa County Court, in Martinez, California, Polk accused the judge, the prosecutors, the police, and many others of having a conspiracy against her. She maintained that the crime scene was tampered with and went on to say that she is a psychic and foresaw the September 11, 2001 terrorist attacks.[273]

It should be noted that in 2001 Susan Polk filed for divorce. It was a very bitter divorce, and she left their house and moved to Montana. Felix Polk was given custody of their youngest son and retained sole control of their house. Susan Polk was very angry and disappointed with the court decision and it was reported that Felix told his friends and the police that Susan was threatening to kill him, and a few weeks later his body was found.[274]

Their three sons testified at the trial. On the one hand, two sons, Adam and Gabriel testified against their mother, who they described as being abusive, delusional, and had said on several occasions that she will kill their father. Gabriel was the youngest and 15 years old at the time. Eli was 20 years, and Adam was the oldest. Eli on the other hand testified that his father was violent, abusive, and a batterer. "The testimony by Eli bordered on the bizarre, and provided a window for people to observe the unnaturally close relationship between Susan Polk and her son, leading many to speculate about an incestuous relationship between the two."[275] Prosecutors argued that Susan murdered her husband in order to control the $2 million estate. Susan argued that she acted in self-defense.

During the trial Susan Polk stated that she was a medium and should be believed. She asked the court to allow her to call psychic Annette Martin as an expert witness to testify that psychics/mediums are real. The prosecution argued that Polk was suffering from delusions and resorts to violence. Judge Laurel Brady allowed psychic Annette Martin to testify in court. However, the judge stated that Martin should only say what she did for a living and should not say anything about the scientific underpinnings of her work.[276] The judge got it wrong in this case as Martin should not have been allowed to testify. In Martinez, California, the jury, on June 16, 2006, found Susan Polk guilty of second-degree murder. She received a prison sentence of 16 years to life.

Susan Polk appealed her conviction. Among many claims, Polk argued that there was misconduct by the trial judge, the prosecutor and the jury during the trial. In their ruling, the First District Court of Appeal, San Francisco, stated that the statements made by the jurors at the post-verdict news conference criticizing Polk's behavior during the trial did not show any bias that could have affected the outcome of the case.[277] The First District Court of Appeal also stated that Judge Laurel Brady did not err and that she properly limited the jury's consideration of voluntary manslaughter as an alternative to a murder conviction.[278] The first District Court of Appeal, therefore, upheld her conviction.

Susan Polk filed a petition for a writ of habeas corpus. At the United States District Court for the Northern District of California, Polk argued that "her conviction is constitutionally infirm, that the state courts have wrongly rejected her challenges to her state trial and appellate proceedings, and that she was wrongly denied bail pending appeal."[279] Judge Maxine M. Chesney stated that:

> Under principles of comity and federalism, a federal court should not interfere with ongoing state criminal proceedings by granting injunctive or declaratory relief absent extraordinary circumstances. See Younger v. Harris, 401 U.S. 37, 43-46, 91 S. Ct. 746, 27 L. Ed. 2d 669 (1971); see also Carden v. Montana, 626 F.2d 82, 84 (9th Cir.1980) (applying Younger to habeas petition challenging state pretrial proceedings). Younger abstention is required when: (1) state proceedings, judicial in nature, are pending; (2) the state proceedings involve important state interests; and (3) the state proceedings afford adequate opportunity to raise the constitutional issues. See Middlesex County Ethics Comm. v. Garden State Bar Ass'n, 457 U.S. 423, 432, 102 S. Ct. 2515, 73 L. Ed. 2D 116 (1982). The rationale of Younger applies throughout appellate proceedings, requiring state appellate review of a state court judgment be completed before federal court intervention is permitted. See Huffman v. Pursue, Ltd., 420 U.S. 592, 607-11, 95 S. Ct. 1200, 43 L. Ed. 2d 482 91975); Dubinka v. Judges of the Superior Court, 23 F.3d 218, 223 (9th Cir. 1994) (holding Younger abstention

applies where state appellate remedies have not been exhausted with respect to challenge to criminal conviction).[280]

Judge Chesney dismissed the case and said that, "The dismissal is without prejudice to petitioner's filings a new federal habeas petition once her state criminal proceedings are completed and she has exhausted state court remedies concerning all claims she wishes to raise in federal court."[281] The case reached the California Supreme Court, which, on March 30, 2011, rejected the appeal by Polk challenging her conviction and the lower courts' rulings.

2.7 CONCLUSION

It is submitted that psychics should be used in crime investigations. However, psychics should not be allowed to testify in court because their method lacks adequate foundation as to be introduced into the courtroom as evidence. Their method has not reached the level of reliability and validity required for courtroom use. The method is not generally accepted as being reliable. There are question marks regarding its scientific basis. In fact, the discipline of parapsychology is generally seen as a pseudoscience, even though a method or technique does not have to be scientific to be admissible. As I stated earlier, courts tend to favor new methods or techniques that have undergone some sort of laboratory test.

Presently, the method of using psychics in crime investigations is not reliable, but this does not mean that they cannot assist the police in investigations. In fact, polygraph is not a reliable technique, yet it is still being used by the police to assist them in their investigations. Furthermore, hypnosis, which fundamentally alters an individual's state of mind, has been used in crime investigations and has even been admitted in some courts. Some police departments spend money on other untested approaches to crime, such as property marking and the use of media to effect attitude change. The question becomes—why not on psychics?

Another reason justifying the use of psychics is that in some cases, experienced crime scene investigators can predict criminals based on their intuition and on the crime scene characteristics. Thus, psychics arguably can be placed on the same level as crime scene analysts and psychological profilers.

The future of using psychics in crime investigation looks interesting. It is my belief that eventually the method of using psychics in crime investigations will be widely accepted as another viable investigative tool. It is submitted that those in law enforcement should openly acknowledge their use of psychics, especially in cases where psychics played a major role in solving a crime. I support the idea put forward by Hibbard, Worring, and Brennan that police departments should have properly written guidelines on the use of psychics. One question that deserves further research is the question of whether psychic abilities can be used to detect when somebody is telling the truth or lying. In the final analysis, there are more reasons supporting the use of psychics in crime investigation than reasons not to use them. In the future, psychic testimony may be more applicable and useful in criminal cases than in civil cases.

CHAPTER 3
PERSONALIZING FIREARMS

3.1 INTRODUCTION

> In the field of injury prevention, the modification of products often can be more successful in reducing the incidence and severity of injuries than attempted modifications of behaviors. The automobile is a commonly cited example of the safety benefits associated with product modification. Design changes such as airbags, shatterproof windshields, seatbelts, and collapsible steering columns have all been credited with reducing motor vehicle fatalities. The value of product design interventions probably applies to guns, although to date there have not been adequate product modifications or available data to allow for a full test of the hypothesis.[282]

In recent years, there has been a steady decrease in motor vehicle injuries and this has been attributed to the improvements on the design and marketing of motor vehicles.[283] Many scholars and also public health professionals have called for the application of such safety measures to firearms. Personalizing firearms will help prevent and reduce firearms injuries and deaths. Personalizing firearms involves designing guns with personalized identification technology so that only the authorized user(s) can fire the gun. Despite the fact that the idea of personalizing guns is not new, it still has not been adopted by some of the firearm manufacturers. Furthermore, there are still no federal laws mandating the use of such devices in the design of firearms manufactured in the United States. This chapter examines the reasons for this neglect, and argues that biometrics has a very important role to play in our efforts to prevent and reduce firearm-related injuries and deaths. A critical analysis of the different methods of personalizing guns has been presented and I have addressed such questions as:

1. what are the major advantages and disadvantages of adopting personalized identification systems;
2. are personalized identification technology systems cost effective;
3. are there ways that can be used to "beat" this system;
4. and why are personalized identification technology systems not being used despite the fact that the idea is not new?

Personalized identification technology involves using forms of biometrics or magnetic devices in the design of guns in order to prevent unauthorized use of the gun. This is aimed at preventing unintentional firearm deaths and injuries. Guns can also be personalized using mechanical devices. Personalized identification technology requires a gun owner "to wear a programmable electronic or magnetic ring on the hand that grips the gun or equipping the firearm with a device that recognizes the fingerprints of the authorized user."[284] The idea of personalizing guns started when there were serious concerns about the rising number of police officers being shot with their own guns by criminals. This led to the idea that these deaths could have been prevented if guns were personalized. The need to prevent unintentional deaths and injuries, especially in children and adolescents also led to the great interest in personalizing guns. It should be noted that:

> In 1998, an estimated 13,698 people in the United States (5.1 per 100,000) were treated in hospital emergency departments for nonfatal, unintentionally inflicted gunshot wounds-approximately 16 surviving victims for every fatality. The same data source reveals that, for every four people treated for nonfatal gun assaults, there was one gun homicide, and for every four gun suicides, one person received

> treatment for a self-inflicted gunshot wound. Unintentional firearm injuries, which are generally much less lethal than intentionally inflicted gunshot wounds, accounted in 1998 for 21% of all nonfatal injuries treated in hospital emergency rooms.[285]

There is evidence to suggest that unintentional gun death rates tend to be higher in adolescents aged 10-19, living in nonmetropolitan areas.[286] Majority of unintentional firearm injuries and deaths in urban areas are caused by handguns; most likely to occur in the home or near the home, and usually occur when handling or playing with the gun.[287] One study in Kansas City, Missouri, however, found that most unintentional gun injuries in Kansas City took place in the street or in a car while the hand gun was being concealed.[288] Generally, males and rural residents have higher rates of gun ownership and also higher rates of unintentional firearm deaths than females and urban residents.[289] Some studies have also indicated a close association between unintentional gun injuries and rural hunting lifestyle.[290] A study by Sinauer et al. showed that the majority of unintentional nonfatal firearm-related injuries "often occur during common gun-related activities such as gun cleaning, loading/unloading, hunting, target shooting, and showing, handling, or carrying."[291]

3.2 DIFFERENT WAYS OF PERSONALIZING FIREARMS

Electronic Locks

There are many ways of personalizing firearms. The first involves fitting firearms with in-built electronic locks, which enables the user to lock or unlock the gun using a personal identification number (PIN). The main criticism of this device is the fact that some people might forget the PIN in an emergency. These types of guns are already in the market. Firearms can also be personalized by adding mechanical locks to them. This involves the gun trigger being equipped with an in-built lock with a key or combination lock. "These devices are relatively effective as a means of storage because they are difficult to remove without the key or combination, and most people would find it troublesome to shoot the gun with the lock in place."[292] The use of mechanical locks has however, been criticized because the unlocking process is slow and will be a problem in an emergency.[293] This type of firearm has been produced and has been in the market since 1970.

Designing Firearms with Fingerprint Sensors

The second and most interesting way of personalizing firearms involves the design of firearms with sensors on the trigger that will recognize the fingerprint of the authorized user before the gun can be fired. This device will bc fast and will solve the major problems associated with the other methods. Sensors can recognize fingerprints in seconds. If police officers are to use this type of device, then the manufacturers must ensure that the sensors can work even when someone is wearing gloves as most police officers do for health and safety reasons. Colt Company is reported to have received a grant from the Federal government for research and development of this type of device. Taurus International Manufacturing is also partnering with the New Jersey Institute of Technology in developing such guns.

Radio Frequency Identification Device

Equipping guns with Radio Frequency Identification Device (RFID) is also another way of personalizing guns. This involves the use of radio waves and an in-built antenna on the gun. With this device, "the waves are transmitted from a ring or wristband worn by the shooter. The gun would be capable of accepting several memory codes; this would be helpful for families that have more than one authorized user."[294]

There have been concerns on the reliability of this sort of device. Power failure, interaction with other radio equipment, bad antenna reception, interference with other wireless devices and distance are serious concerns.[295] It has also been argued that some people might forget to wear the ring or the wristband.[296] It is important to point out the following:

> While officers could probably be trained to include this new gadget as part of their daily equipment checks, civilians may have more difficult time remembering to grab their gun-watchband/ring as they chase burglars from their homes. As a practical matter, some persons keeping a loaded gun in the home would also keep the unlocking device similarly close to the firearm. While this would decrease the time necessary to make the gun operable, it would also substantially undermine the goals of personalization since everything necessary to use the gun would be in one place.[297]

It has been noted that burglars and other individuals would simply steal both the gun and the RFID.[298] Colt Company is reported to have manufactured a prototype of this sort. As we can see from the above discussion, equipping guns with radio frequency identification devices raises several serious issues. The fact that the radio reception can be lost when needed is a big concern. There is also the tendency for some people to forget to wear the wristband or ring, especially in an emergency at night while the person has been sleeping. If you put the wrist band or the ring next to the gun, then the main purpose of using the device is defeated. Battery failure is also another concern, though this can be solved. This option is not supported.

Tarnhelm Supply Co. Inc. has produced what they have called "Magna-Trigger Gun Safety," which works with a magnetic ring. It is only when the ring is worn that the gun can fire. The ring contains a magnet. The cost of adding the Magna-Trigger conversion device to a handgun is $350 and the ring costs $60.[299] This device has been developed for Smith & Wesson J, K, L, and N frame guns, as well as for Ruger Security Six gun.[300] According to Tarnhelm Company:

Guns have been modified for police since June, 1976. For convenience, all magnetic rings allow firing of all modified guns. The device slides out for easy gun cleaning, and never requires oiling. Only one moving part is employed. The device is expected to outlast your gun by countless years. The powerful samarium magnets can last for centuries. The tiny stainless steel rings never tarnish, and weigh only five grams (1/5 ounce). You wear the ring on your middle finger for the six-shot guns and on the ring finger for the five-shot guns or the Ruger. Most officers wear a ring on both hands.[301]

Firearms with Remote Control

Another way of personalizing guns is through the use of a remote control device to operate the gun, "in which a small hand-held transmitter would enable or disable a firearm. While the device would require positive human action for its operation, it would be transferable to other persons. As with the RFID technology, there would be the constant threat of battery failure issue and interference with other radio waves."[302] In my view, the issue of battery failure is not a serious problem, because the device can be fitted with a beeping device that indicates when the battery is low. This has been proven to work in carbon monoxide detectors and smoke alarms. Leonardatos et al. were highly critical of operating firearms with remote controls and argued that there is likely to be the temptation to keep the remote control close to the gun because most people keep their television remote control next to the television.[303] As a result, the burglar will steal both the gun and the remote control.[304] The disadvantages of using remote controls to operate guns far outweigh the advantages. Another serious concern is that one can mistakenly use the firearms remote control thinking that it is the remote control for the television, video, or other electronic equipment. This problem is compounded by the fact that there is now one-for-all or universal remote controls that can be used to operate almost all electronic equipment.

Designing Firearms with a Touch Memory Pad

Designing firearms with a touch memory pad has also been suggested. This form of personalizing firearms is:

> Similar to the radio frequency device, the touch memory device involves a ring or some other item that is capable of being read by the gun. The gun will work only if a particular spot on the gun is touched by a particular spot on the ring. The advantage of this invention is that when it works properly, the reading is fast enough to satisfy most police or other defense needs. The touch memory does require an electronic connection, making it dependent upon a power source with all the accompanying complications. In addition to the problem of power supply, the reading could be impaired not only by a user's gloves, but by dirt, blood, sweat, and oil. (Oil is used to clean guns, and a clean gun may have some residual oil).[305]

This option has also faced criticism. One of the main problems with this option is that there must be precise alignment of the bar code before the memory pad can operate. This is a serious concern during emergencies. During emergencies, precision may not be possible because of several factors, such as the individual panicking.[306]Therefore, personalized guns must be designed so that the guns can be fired in all environmental conditions, such as heat, rain, fog, mud, sand, snow, and perspiration.[307]

3.3 ADVANTAGES AND DISADVANTAGES OF PERSONALIZING FIREARMS

One of the major advantages of personalizing guns is that it helps in preventing unintentional deaths and injuries, especially in children and adolescents. It limits access to firearms by unauthorized users, especially children and adolescents who use them to commit suicide and homicide. As we have seen in this book, several studies have shown that many children and adolescents are killed or injured while handling their parents' loaded firearms without permission. Therefore, personalizing guns is a step in the right direction. Allied to the above is the fact that by personalizing guns, the risk of law enforcement officers being shot by their own guns is removed. It has also been noted that by personalizing guns that the number of guns stolen will be reduced, since the guns cannot be used by unauthorized persons. In my view though, there is likely to be a shift on the reasons why guns are stolen. This time criminals will not steal guns to use them in crime, but will steal them to sell for recycling. The metals and chips in guns can be bought and recycled. The only problem is ascertaining if the cost is worth it. Criminals can also move into exporting these guns to other countries where the metals and chips will probably have higher values. Suffice it to say, therefore, that personalizing guns will probably not result in a significant reduction in the theft of firearms, unless the firearms are manufactured with materials that are worthless or not of high value if melted/recycled. The most obvious disadvantage of personalizing firearms is that it will lead to an increase in the cost.

> A concern for police departments is the cost of the technology. The goal for police as set by Sandia Labs was that the invention should add no more than $60 to the cost of a gun and no more than $5 to the annual maintenance costs. Manufacturers, however, who have developed or who are in the process of developing personalization technology, claim that the costs for their products would be between $100-$400. As the Wall Street Journal noted, "the cost and reliability of smart guns are very much in doubt." The additional cost could negatively impact the budget of a small police department.[308]

Some scholars have argued that if personalized guns are made mandatory that poor people will not be able to afford them, which raises questions as to whether this amounts to denial of equal protection for poor people.[309] However, it has been noted that technological advances may lead to a reduction of the cost of firearms in the future.[310] Leonardatos et al. argued that "the prospect of a future decline in costs does not erase the present effect of making it nearly impossible for poor people to exercise constitutional rights."[311] In my opinion, the law does not state that guns must be sold at a particular base price. It is not compulsory that every citizen must own a gun in many jurisdictions. Gun ownership is not a social amenity that must be provided by the state. Law enforcement agencies are charged with the constitutional duty of protecting the citizens. The United States law enforcement agents are undoubtedly one of the most highly trained and well-equipped agencies in the world. The argument by some scholars that an increase in the cost of personalized guns amounts to denial of equal protection to poor people is simply an overreaction. Gun ownership is more of an individual choice at the moment. We should also not forget that the correct meaning and interpretation of the Second Amendment is still debatable. Even though the United States Supreme Court has addressed the issue, the Court still left some questions unanswered.

It appears that if personalized guns are shown to prevent unintentional deaths and injuries, the increased costs will probably not be a major problem to the public. In fact, two national surveys aimed at ascertaining public opinion on innovative gun-policy options indicated that a great number of people support personalization of guns.[312] Teret et al. conducted two telephone surveys of 1,200 adults each in the United States in 1996 and 1997-1998, and found that "a majority of the respondents favored safety standards for new handguns. These standards included childproofing (favored by 88 percent of respondents), personalization (devices that permit firing only by an authorized person; 71 percent), magazine safeties (device that prevent firing after the magazines or clip is removed; 82 percent), and loaded-chamber indicators (devices that show whether the handgun is loaded; 73 percent)."[313] The two surveys are remarkable, because they specifically informed the respondents that "personalized guns will cost more than other guns, and the chances that the gun will not fire when you want it may be increased slightly."[314] Yet, and interestingly, "71 percent of those surveyed favored a law requiring personalization, and among gun owners, 59 percent favored such a law."[315] Other surveys have supported this position. For instance, a survey of 1,204 adults in the 50 states indicated that 95.8 percent will support a policy requiring The United States made firearms to meet the same quality standards as imported firearms, even if this will lead to an increase in the cost of firearms.[316] It should be noted that few states have passed laws that requires guns sold in the states to have some sort of personalizing device.[317]

3.4 COUNTERMEASURES

Having examined the advantages and disadvantages of personalizing guns, the question becomes: Are there ways that criminals can "beat" the methods of personalizing guns? Unfortunately, there are ways that can be used to beat some of the personalization devices. Leonardatos et al. notes:

> In the gun industry, such efforts by an owner to defeat personalization are called "chip twigglies." Among the obvious methods, depending upon the particular personalization device, are: removing the personalization equipment; removing the battery; allowing the battery to die; destroying the magnetic images; cooking the gadget to expose it to extreme heat; and gluing the button to maintain the unlock position. Most of these evasion techniques could also be accomplished by criminals intending to use a stolen gun later.[318]

Leonardatos et al. also noted that personalization can be "beaten" by simply leaving the personalization device enabled all the time.[319]

3.5 WHY IS PERSONALIZED IDENTIFICATION TECHNOLOGY NOT BEING USED?

Why is personalized identification technology not being used despite the fact that the idea is not new? This can be attributed to the fact that some of the gun manufacturers are not in support of personalizing guns. Glock Company, for instance, has been reluctant to get involved in personalizing guns. This is compounded by the federal government's indifference to the idea of regulating the design of domestically manufactured guns. Commenting on the need for legislative and litigated interventions, Frattaroli et al. maintained that:

> In the absence of voluntary installation of safety devices by gun manufacturers, one can look to legislation and litigation as means to compel gun makers to produce safer guns. Historically, the federal government has not regulated guns and their manufacturers with regard to public safety. Congress expressly forbade the Consumer Product Commission from exercising any jurisdiction over guns and ammunition. The Bureau of Alcohol, Tobacco, and Firearms within the Treasury Department does not regulate the safe design of guns. Thus, although guns are a ubiquitous and dangerous consumer product, guns are unlike other consumer products in that their design is not subject to regulation for the benefit of the public's safety."[320]

It has been noted, however, that legislative mandates requiring people to buy personalized guns could lead many people into ignoring safe gun handling and storage practices.[321] This argument merits further research.

In their own contribution on the reasons why the idea of personalizing firearms in order to protect the public has not been seriously implemented, Teret et al. also noted that this could be because the design and safety of handguns are unregulated and has been left primarily to manufacturers.[322]Wayne believes that personalization of guns has not become a reality because the process is very complicated.[323]

Another reason why personalizing guns has not fully come to fruition is the fact that the National Rifle Association (NRA), the most powerful pro-gun lobbying group in the United States is not in support of personalizing guns. Wayne LaPierre, executive vice president of the NRA, believes that firearm victims could not have been saved by such personalized devices and he said, "They could have been saved by something far simpler and more common sense, zero-tolerance enforcement of the mandatory sentencing provisions in the gun laws against violent criminals we've had on the books for a long time."[324]

Furthermore, some scholars have argued that personalized guns are unreliable. Hence, some manufacturers are taking their time in research and development of personalizing devices to make sure that they do not fail the reliability tests. Metcalf contended that there is no room for error when it comes to designing personalized guns, arguing that "if you swipe your ATM card and it doesn't read it, do it again. But if you reach for your gun to defend yourself and it doesn't recognize your identification, you don't get a second chance."[325]

3.6 CONCLUSION

After a critical evaluation of the different ways of personalizing firearms, it appears that fitting fingerprint sensors on the trigger solves most of the problems inherent in the other methods. There will be no delays in using the guns. Sensors can recognize fingerprints in a matter of seconds. Even if the sensors use battery, battery failure can be solved by including a low battery beeper in the design. Another advantage of using this type of device is that it does not require the user to wear any wristband or ring, which he or she can forget. Moreover, guns are not used every day by civilians for defensive purposes. It is therefore submitted that equipping the trigger of firearms with sensors that can identify the authorized user through fingerprint is the best option.

When it comes to preventing and reducing the rates of unintentional deaths and injuries, personalizing firearms will have significant positive effects, but there are doubts as to whether personalization of guns will have any positive impact on solving the problem of straw purchases. The absence of federal laws regulating the design of domestically manufactured firearms is a serious problem. This book, therefore, supports the idea of establishing a federal agency to regulate the design of firearms. Taking a costs-benefits approach, it is submitted that the benefits of personalizing firearms will far outweigh the costs. Based on the above issues and other factors, I conclude that using personalized identification technology to prevent firearms injuries is justified.

CHAPTER 4
CONFRONTING THE NIGERIAN 419 E-MAIL SCAM

4.1 INTRODUCTION

The 419 scam is a transnational organized crime. It is operated through criminal cells. In recent times, with the widespread availability of communications technology, especially the internet, the 419 scam is now increasingly being initiated through e-mails. It should be noted that individuals as well as companies, churches, and organizations are all targets of 419 scams. The 419 scams, however, are most likely to succeed with individuals as opposed to companies. This can be explained by the fact that in companies, more than one person is involved in making decisions on business deals and proposals. The scam is therefore likely to be detected by one of the company executives.

Despite the fact that billions of dollars have been siphoned out of many people throughout the world, especially in western countries, the 419 scam still continues. There are indications that 419 scam losses have reached billions of dollars.[326] The 419 scam is not new. It is therefore, worrying that it is still continuing. In this chapter, the following questions have been addressed: Why Nigerians? Who falls for these scams? Are some victims to be blamed? Can the United States stop this scam? And most importantly, what is to be done to stop the Nigerian 419 Scam? In order to answer these questions, there has been a critical examination of some of the 419 scam letters, as well as an examination of the social-economic background of some of the victims. This book concludes that some of the victims are to be blamed, calls for the prosecution of some of these victims and makes suggestions on how to solve this scam.

The main argument of this chapter is that in almost all the 419 scam letters the criminal intent is clear. Therefore, victims of such cases where the criminal intent is obvious should be prosecuted. We need to put in place measures to discourage people from getting involved in these scams. One way is to make it an offense in all jurisdictions/countries. United States citizens need to be made aware that it is a federal crime to participate in foreign lottery scams.

4.2 WHAT IS 419 SCAM?

The 419 scam is a transnational organized crime carried out through e-mails, telephone, mail, and fax; it usually involves an invitation to transfer money, offer of travel, or a request for business partnership, and in return you are told that you will get a certain percentage of money. The 419 scam is by and large carried out mainly by Nigerians. The Nigerian 419 scam arguably started in the 1970s but skyrocketed in the 1980s following the widespread availability of the internet. This rise has also been attributed to the drop in oil prices, which consequently led to high unemployment in Nigeria. It should be noted, however, that the first recorded scam of this nature occurred in Spain in 1588, in what is commonly referred to as the Spanish Prisoner Scam. In this scam, it was reported that a wealthy Englishman was being held captive by Phillip XI of Spain and some wealthy Englishmen were approached to give money to help release the prisoner. The potential victims were told that "The investor that paid the prisoner's ransom would be amply rewarded financially, as well as getting the prisoner's beautiful and worried young daughter in marriage. Individuals who accepted the offer paid for one failed rescue attempt after another, with the fictitious prisoner continuing to languish in his nonexistent dungeon, always just one more bribe away from being released."[327]

4.3 FORMS OF 419 SCAM

There are many forms of the 419 scam. Potential victims are located through various means, including public records, internet searches, mailing lists, telephone records, and conference records. The 419 scammers arc people who will use any situation or event in order to scam people. The various forms of the 419 scam include the advance fee fraud, the winning lottery scam, dating scam, next of kin/inheritance scam, overpayment scam, laundering crooked money scam, and black money scam.

Advance Fee Scam

Highly educated professionals tend to fall for advance fee scam as opposed to the other types. The victims usually ignore several warnings from family, friends, and law enforcement agents. Greed is the key factor that drives many people into this kind of scam. Below are examples of advance fee scam letters. Please note that these scam letters contain many errors. This is a deliberate ploy by the scammers aimed at deceiving people.

> Confidential Transaction!
> From:Mr. Hazim Hussan
> (hazimhussan1960@gmail.com)
> Sent: Sat 1/15/11 8:44 PM
>
> Dear Friend,
>
> I am Mr.Hazim Hussan, I work with the Bill & Exchange department African Development Bank (ADB) Ouagadougou Burkina Faso. I have a business which will be beneficial to both of us? The amount of money involved is ($20.5 Million US Dollars) which i want to transfer out of the country to you're bank account, all to my financial benefit and yours too.
>
> This money is owned by a man called MR.KATTAN SHERIF a business commercialist in west-African regions. He has been dead since six years ago and since then no claim has been placed on his bank

account balance. I want to transfer this money out of the country but such fund can not be transferred without a next of kin attached to the fund.

The fund could be transferred in this way; you shall present yourself as business associates to the deceased person [Mr.Kattan Sherif] as details shall be that you are the care-taker business associates to Mr.Kattan Sherif and his properties. I shall make available to you materials and information with which a successful claim shall be placed on the fund. I shall be your guidance and instructor throughout the duration of this transaction so as to ensure a swift and sure transfer of the fund to your bank account.

As to your benefits, you shall be entitled to 40% of this fund for your co-operation in this transaction while 5% will be set aside for expenses both of us incurred during the course of this transaction. so if you are interested, please treat this business with utmost confidentiality and call me for more talks.

Please this business must strictly be a deal between both of us and feel free to call me on my Private Telephone No. 00226 76 371721.

Take note that both of us will incur any expense occur. If you are capable and ready indicate your willingness by sending the under listed informations:

(1)Your Full Name:
(2)Your age.
(3)Your occupation
(4)Your marital status
(5)Your full residential address.
(6)Your direct phone and fax numbers.
(7)Your Country of Origin:

Kind regards,

From Mr.Hazim Hussan
Bill & Exchange Manager
African Development Bank (ADB)
Burkina Faso.
Direct Phone No; 00226 76 371721.
PLEASE I NEED YOUR URGENT ASSISTANCE
From: sama issa (sama_issa1@sify.com)
Sent: Wed 9/14/11 9:53 AM
To: ATTENTION:

I am the manager in file and computer department of BANK OF AFRICA I got your contact through international business inquiry as i was desperately searching for a honest foreigner who will help me receive this abandoned money in his account.

In my department i discovered a file of unclaimed fund of $12.250m US dollars (TWELVE MILLION TWO HUNDRED AND FIFTY THOUSAND US DOLLARS). In an account that belongs to one of our foreign customer who died along with his entire family in plane crash 2003. Since we got information about his death, we have been expecting his next of kin to come over and claim his money because we cannot release it unless somebody applies for it as next of kin or relation to the deceased as indicated in our banking guidelines but unfortunately we learnt that all his supposed next of kin or relation died alongside with him at the plane crash leaving nobody behind for the claim.

It is therefore upon this discovery that I now decided to make this business proposal to you and release the money to you as the next of kin or relation to the deceased for safety and subsequent disbursement since nobody is coming for it and I don't want this money to go into the Bank treasury as unclaimed Bill.The Banking law and guideline here stipulates that if such money remained unclaimed after ten years, the money will be transfer into the Bank treasury as unclaimed fund. The request of foreigner as next of kin in this business is occasioned by the fact that the customer was a foreigner and a Burkinabe cannot stand as next of kin to a foreigner.

I agree that 30% of this money will be for you as foreign partner, in respect to the provision of a foreign account, 10% will be set aside for expenses incurred during the business and 60% would be for me. There after I will visit your country for disbursement according to the percentages indicated. Therefore to enable the immediate transfer of this fund to you as arranged, you must apply first to the bank as relations or next of kin of the deceased indicating your bank name, your bank account number, your private telephone and fax number for easy and effective communication and location where in the money will be remitted.

I will not fail to bring to your notice that this transaction is hitch free and that you should not entertain any atom of fear as all required arrangements have been made for the transfer. Once more, i assure you that nobody will ask of this fund after the fund has successfully been transferred to your account and i will not forget to tell you that every information regarding to the deceased customer including the information backing his account are all intact with me, so you should be rest assured that i have done my home work very well before contacting you.

You should contact me immediately as soon as you receive this letter. Trusting to hear from you immediately.

Yours Sincerely,

Mr.sama issa

The Winning Lottery Scam

The winning lottery scam operates as follows: You will receive an email from the scammer saying that you are a winner in a lottery draw and that your email was randomly selected. You will be given details of the person to contact for processing your lottery win. The email may contain a website where you will be asked to confirm the winning. A typical winning lottery email will contain two email addresses: one where it is sent from, and one where you are told to respond to. You are also asked to give personal identifying information.

Many people are not aware that participation in foreign lottery is a federal crime in the United States. United States Code: Title 18, 1953. Interstate transportation of wagering paraphernalia makes it an offense to participate in cross-border sale or purchase of foreign lottery tickets by mail or by phone. The Code states as follows:

(a) Whoever, except a common carrier in the usual course of its business, knowingly carries or sends in interstate or foreign commerce any record, paraphernalia, ticket, certificate, bills, slip, token, paper, writing, or other device used, or to be used, or adapted, devised, or designed for use in (a) bookmaking; or (b) wagering pools with respect to a sporting event; or (c) in a numbers, policy, bolita, or similar game shall be fined under this title or imprisoned for not more than five years or both.

(b) This section shall not apply to:

(1) parimutuel betting equipment, parimutuel tickets where legally acquired, or parimutuel materials used or designed for use at racetracks or other sporting events in connection with which betting is legal under applicable State law, or

(2) the transportation of betting materials to be used in the placing of bets or wagers on a sporting event into a State in which such betting is legal under the statutes of that State, or

(3) the carriage or transportation in interstate or foreign commerce of any newspaper or similar publication, or

(4) equipment, tickets, or materials used or designed for use within a State in a lottery conducted by that State acting under authority of State law, or

(5) the transportation in foreign commerce to a destination in a foreign country of equipment, tickets, or materials designed to be used within that foreign country in a lottery which is authorized by the laws of that foreign country.

(c) Nothing contained in this section shall create immunity from criminal prosecution under any laws of any State, Commonwealth of Puerto Rico, territory, possession, or the District of Columbia.

(d) For the purposes of this section (1) "State" means a State of the United States, the District of Columbia, the Commonwealth of Puerto Rico, or any territory or possession of the United States; and (2) "foreign country" means any empire, county, dominion, colony, or protectorate, or any subdivision thereof (other than the United States, its territories or possessions).

(e) For the purposes of this section "lottery" means the pooling of proceeds derived from the sale of tickets or chances and allotting those proceeds or parts thereof by chance to one or more takers or ticket purchasers. "Lottery" does not include the placing or accepting of bets or wagers on sporting events or contests.[328]

The Federal Trade Commission cautions any person thinking of participating in foreign lottery to note that:

> If you play a foreign lottery—through the mail or over the telephone—you're violating federal law. There are no secret systems for winning foreign lotteries. Your chances of winning more than the cost of your tickets are slim to none. If

> you purchase one foreign lottery ticket, expect many more bogus offers for lottery or investment 'opportunities.' Your name will be placed on 'sucker lists' that fraudulent telemarketers buy and sell. Keep your credit card and bank account numbers to yourself. Scam artists often ask for them during an unsolicited sales pitch.[329]

The message is clear—do not reply to these international lottery solicitations.

Money Transfer

Another more common form of the 419 scam is the request for assistance to transfer money. Victims of this type of scam should be watched and investigated. Under this type of scam, the potential victim is asked to assist in transferring a large sum of money out of a country in exchange for some percentage of the amount. This is money laundering and should be taken seriously. See below an example of such solicitations. As you can see from this letter, the criminal intent is obvious.

> Confidential
>
> From: Joseph Dinga-dzondo (josephdzondo@gmail.com) Sent: Mon 9/05/11 10:40 AM
> To:
> FROM THE DESK OF JOSEPH DINGA-DZONDO
> THE AUDITING AND ACCOUNTING SECTION MANAGER WITH AFRICAN DEVELOPMENT BANK, (A.D.B.) OUAGADOUGOU BURKINA FASO.
>
> Dear Friend,
> I know that this message will come to you as a surprise. I am Joseph Dinga -Dzondo, the Auditing and Accounting section manager with African Development Bank, Ouagadougou Burkina faso. I Hope that you will not expose or betray this trust and confident that

I am about to repose on you for the mutual benefit of our both families.

I need your urgent assistance in transferring the sum of ($39.5) Million Dollars only to your account within 10 or 14 banking days. This money has been dormant for years in our Bank without claim.I want the bank to release the money to you as the nearest person to our deceased customer late Mr.George Small who died along with his supposed next of kin in an air crash since 31st October 1999.

I don't want the money to go into government treasury as an abandoned fund. So this is the reason why I am contacting you so that the bank can release the money to you as the next of kin to the deceased customer. Please I would like you to keep this proposal as a top secret and delete it if you are not interested.

Upon receipt of your reply, I will give you full details on how the business will be executed and also note that you will have 40% of the above mentioned sum if you agree to handle this business with me.

I am expecting your urgent response as soon as you receive my message.
Best Regard,
Mr Joseph.

Next of Kin

Allied to the money transfer scam is the next of kin or inheritance scam. Typically, the letter will ask you to lie and agree to be the next of kin. Usually, the letter will state that they have information about a dormant bank account or the account holder has died and a next of kin is needed to claim the money. If you agree to stand in as the next of kin, you are guaranteed a certain percentage of the money.

The criminal intent in this type of the 419 scam is also very clear as you can see in the letter below.

HELLO DEAR,

From: Mrs. Rahina Azmi,

I'm the head of International remittance department CIMB BANK Malaysia; I got your contact from global worldwide research, as l need a foreign business partner. To execute a DEAL of (19, 000,000.00 US Dollars) with me. it has already arranged but i am looking for a foreigner who will be Capable to handle it with me.

If you are capable please update me immediately, I will introduce you to my bank as the relative to the late customer who deposited the fund in our Bank, and the fund will be transfer to you in your country, this our customer dead with his family. i will send you the information of this our late customer that will make you understand this business, no risk involved. As all the legal documents to transfer the fund to you will be in your name. And them we will discus what will be your percentage. This business will be executed under a legitimate arrangement with me from the Bank.

I will appreciate you're immediately respond to my personal Email: mrs.rahinaazmi@azet.sk

Yours Sincerely,
Mrs. Rahina Azmi.

Overpayment

This type of scam also shows a high degree of criminal intent. Below is an example of such letters.

From: ROBERT S. MUELLER
(mail44@w52dp9m1v.homepage.t-online.de) Sent:
Mon 9/05/11 7:13 PM
To:
Federal Bureau of Investigation
Counter-terrorism Division and Cyber Crime
Division
J. Edgar. Hoover Building Washington DC
FBI HEADQUARTERS IN WASHINGTON D.C.
FEDERAL BUREAU OF INVESTIGATION
J. EDGAR HOOVER BUILDING

Attention Beneficiary,
Re: Funds Release Notification
Records show that you are among one of the individuals and organizations who are yet to receive their overdue payment from overseas which includes those of Lottery/Gambling, Contract and Inheritance. Through our Fraud Monitory Unit we have also noticed that over the past you have been transacting with some impostors and fraudsters who have been impersonating the likes of Prof. Soludo/Mr.Lamido Sanusi of the Central Bank Of Nigeria, Mr. Patrick Aziza, Bode Williams, Frank, Anderson, none officials of Oceanic Bank, Zenith Banks, Kelvin Young of HSBC, Ben of FedEx, Ibrahim Sule, Dr. Usman Shamsuddeen and some impostors claiming to be The Federal Bureau of Investigation.
The Cyber Crime Division of the FBI gathered information from the Internet Fraud Complaint Center (IFCC) of how some people have lost outrageous sums of money to these impostors. As a result of this we hereby advise you to stop communication with any one not referred to you
by us. We have negotiated with the Federal Ministry of Finance that your payment of
$15,000,000.00 will be released to you via ATM card with a maximum withdrawal limit of
$15,000 per day which is powered by Visa Card and can be used anywhere in the world where you see a

Visa Card Logo on the Automatic Teller Machine (ATM). We have advised that this should be the only way at which you are to receive your payment because its more guaranteed, since over $5 billion was lost on fake cheque last year 2010.

We guarantee 100% receipt of your payment, because we have perfected everything in regards to the release of your $15 million United States Dollars to be 100% guarantee free and free from any hitches as its our duty to protect citizens of the United States of America and also Asia and Europe. (This is as a result of the mandate from US Government to make sure all debts owed to citizens of American and also Asia and Europe which includes Inheritance, Contract, Gambling/Lottery etc are been cleared for the betterment of the current economic status of the nation and its citizens as he has always believed, Our Time for Change has come because, Change can happen).Below are few list of tracking numbers you can track from UPS website to confirm people like you who have received their payment successfully.

Name: E LINDBERG:DHL Tracking Number 1426425615 (www.dhl.com) Name :PITELIS :UPS Tracking Number h8433223480 (www.ups.com)
To redeem your fund you are hereby advised to contact the ATM Card Center via email for their requirement to proceed and procure your Approval of Payment Warrant and Endorsement of your ATM Release Order on your behalf which will cost you $295.00 only nothing more and no hidden fees as everything else has been taken cared of by the Federal Government including taxes, custom paper and clearance duty so all you will ever need to pay is $295.00 only.

ATM Visa Card Director Contact Information:
Name:
Email. drlinus_peterson@one.co.il

Or contact Dr. Linus Peterson of the ATM Card Center via his contact details above and furnish him with your details as listed below:
1. Your full
Name: ....
2. Home/Cell
Phone:..
3. Occupation:..
4. Age:...
5. Your Address (where you will like your ATM
CARD to be sent to):..
On contacting him with your details your files would be updated and he will be sending you the payment information in which you will use in making payment of $295.00 via Western Union Money Transfer for the procurement of your Approval of Payment Warrant and Endorsement of your ATM Release Order. After which the delivery of your ATM card will be affected to your designated home address without any further delay, extra fee or any authority raising eyebrow. Upon receipt of payment the delivery officer will ensure that your package is sent within 48 working hours. Because we are so sure of everything we are giving you a 100% money back guarantee if you do not receive your ATM CARD Shipment Confirmation within the next 48hrs after you have made the payment. Once again we are so sure of you receiving your payment at no any other cost as we have taking it upon our duty to monitor everything in other to cub cyber crime that is perpe! trated by those impostors.

Thanks,
ROBERT MUELLER, DIRECTOR: FEDERAL
BUREAU OF INVESTIGATION
UNITED STATES DEPARTMENT OF JUSTICE
WASHINGTON, D.C. 20535

Note: Disregard any email you get from any impostors or offices claiming to be in possession of your ATM card, you are hereby advice only to be in contact with Dr.L.Peterson of the ATM card center who is the rightful person to deal with in regards to your payment and forward any emails you get from impostors to this office so we could act upon it immediately. Help stop cyber crime.

Scammed Victim Beneficiary Scam/Compensation
Below are typical 419 scam letters telling potential victims they are entitled to compensation.

United Nation and Obama Foundation
From:Compensation 2011 (info@unifacs.br) Sent: Sat 1/15/11 2:08 PM
To:
Greetings To You,
We notify you as a scammed victim beneficiary to be compensated with $950, 000.00USD in the United Nation and Obama Foundation
Contact Mr.Peter Kelly For more Information.
You are to fill the appropriate form and submit to the bank.
[1] Full Names:__________
[2] Contact address_________________
[3] Direct Telephone No: _____________
[4] Occupation : ______________
Managing Director of the HSBC BANK,Malaysia
Name: Mr.Peter Kelly
Yours Faithfully,
Hon.Mr.Clow Griff
(Chief Co-ordinator)
OBAMA'S FOUNDATION
Copyright © 2003-2011

INSTANT COMPENSATION PAYMENT VALUED AT USD 1.3 MILLION
11/26/12
Citibank New York
From: Citibank New York (bryanbaker@citibank.com)
Sent: Mon 11/26/12 4:29 PM
To:

It is my modest obligation to write you this letter as regards the authorization of your owed payment through our most respected financial institution (Citibank). I am mr. Bryan Barker, the chief executive officer, foreign operations department Citibank of new York, the British government in conjunction with us government, world bank, united nations organization on foreign payment matters has empowered my bank after much consultation and consideration to handle all foreign payments and release them to their appropriate beneficiaries with the help of a representative from federal reserve bank of new York.
As the newly appointed/accredited international paying bank, we have been instructed by the world governing body together with the committee on international debt reconciliation department to release your overdue funds with immediate effect; with this exclusive vide transaction no.: wha/eur/202, transfer allocation no.: citibank/x44/701ln/wgb/gb, password: 339331, pin code: 78569, immediate Citibank secret code: xxtn014.having received these vital payment numbers, you are instantly qualified to receive and confirm your payment with us within the next 48hrs.
Be informed that we have verified your payment file as directed to us and your name is next on the list of our outstanding fund beneficiaries to receive their payment before the end of this Last term of the year 2012. Be advised that because of too many funds beneficiaries due for payment at this Last quarter of the year, you are entitled to receive the sum of one million three hundred thousand us dollars (1,300,000.00 us dollars) only, as part payment so as to enable us pay other eligible beneficiaries to facilitate with the process of this transaction, please kindly re-confirm the following Information below:
1) Your full name:
2) Your full address:
3) Your contact telephone and Fax:

4) Your Email:
5) Your profession:
6) Any valid form of your identification/driven license:
7) Bank name:
8) Bank address:
9) Account name:
10) Account number:
11) Swift code:
12) Routing number:
As soon as we receive the above mentioned information, your payment will be processed and released to you without any further delay. Be also informed that
You are not allowed to communicate with any other person(s) or office any longer so as to avoid conflict of information, you are required to provide the above information for your transfer to take place through bank to bank transfer directly from Citibank.

We look forward to serving you better.
Mr. Bryan Barker,
Director Wire Transfer Unit

Black Money
The black money scam, also known as dirty money scam, is one of the most ridiculous forms of the 419 scam and also shows criminal intent. Potential victims are told that, "a large sum of money has been treated with a special chemical substance making it unusable; however, another special chemical can be used to clean it. If you front the money to buy the chemical, a healthy commission is waiting for you; but hurry, the chemists aren't willing to make the chemical much longer."[330] The fact that many people are falling for this this type of scam is worrying.

Other Forms of 419 Scam
Other areas to watch out for 419 scams include situations when there are large sporting events, political upheavals, natural disasters, religious disturbances, and air

accidents. Another key area to watch out for is scam letters that will say that a class action suit has been settled and you are one of the beneficiaries. Contact the appropriate agencies immediately if you receive such letters.

4.4 STAGES IN 419 SCAM

There are five stages in the 419 scam process. The first is the *Invitation stage* when you are invited to participate in the scam. The initial letter is usually written to appear that urgent action and confidentiality are needed. The second stage is the *Promises stage* where the scammer outlines in more details your rewards. The third stage is the *Persuasion stage*. Here are more promises and incentives, and you will be told that assistance will be rendered, and that you will be met by top officials, and that you have nothing to worry about. The fourth stage is when the victim has sent in some money and some *Money has been Received*. At this stage you will still be asked to send more money, and told that only one thing stands between you and millions of dollars. Another processing fee will be requested. The fifth stage is the *Threat stage*. This is the most dangerous stage, and there have been reports of some victims who have been murdered, or kidnapped.

4.5 WHY NIGERIANS?

Why is this scam carried out mainly by Nigerians? Poverty, unemployment, and corruption have been put forward by many scholars as some of the reasons why these Nigerians started the 419 scam. It has been observed that:

> Advance Fee Fraud criminals include university-educated professionals who are experts in non-violent but spectacular crimes. Advance Fee Fraud letters first surfaced in the mid-1980s around the time of the collapse of world oil prices, which is Nigeria's main foreign exchange earner. It is believed that some Nigerians turned to crime in order to survive. Fraudulent schemes such as Advance Fee Fraud have succeeded in Nigeria, because Nigerian criminals took advantage of the fact that Nigerians speak English, the international

> language of business, and the country's vast oil wealth and natural gas reserves — ranked 13th in the world – offer lucrative business opportunities that attract many foreign companies and individuals.[331]

The current laws on this scam are not adequate, do not discourage the scammers, and many government officials are involved in this scam.[332] Many of these corrupt government officials obstruct the investigations.[333] Adomi and Igun maintained that inadequate law enforcement, lack of transparency and accountability as well as utter disregard for the rule of law also explains why Nigerians are involved in these scams.[334]

4.6 WHO ARE THE VICTIMS?

Who falls for these scams? Is there a typical profile of individuals who are likely to become victims? There is no typical profile of potential victims, per se. However, anybody who likes to reap where he or she did not sow is likely to become a victim. As Michael Zuckoff has pointed out, "every swindle is driven by a desire for easy money, it's the one thing the swindler and the swindled have in common."[335] Greed is an indicator or key factor. In fact, the United States law enforcement agencies see greed as what prompts a lot of people into getting involved in the 419 scam. The U.S. Department of State noted that "victims range in age from 18 to 81 and come from all socio-economic backgrounds."[336] The FBI noted that "the scheme relies on convincing a willing victim, who has demonstrated a 'propensity for larceny' by responding to the invitation, to send money to the author of the letter in Nigeria in several installments of increasing amounts for a variety of reasons."[337]

The 419 victims can be divided into three types: the innocent victim, the gullible victim, and the greedy victim.[338] The innocent victims of the 419 scam are those who think they are actually pursuing a genuine business, and the gullible victims are those who become victims because of their gullibility.[339] As the name suggests, the greedy victims are simply greedy, dishonest, and know fully well that the proposal is illegal. Suffice it to say, therefore, that this type of victim should be blamed for their 'victimization.'

Millions of people worldwide are victims of various types of fraud. In fact, in 2007, 30.5 million Americans (13.5 percent of U.S adults) were victims of fraud.[340] The 2007 Consumer Fraud Survey by the Federal Trade Commission (FTC) showed that the top 10 frauds are Fraudulent Weight-loss Products (4.8 million victims); Foreign Lottery Scams (3.2 million victims); Unauthorized Billing—Buyers Clubs (3.2 million victims); Prize Promotions (2.7 million victims); Work-at-Home Programs (2.4 million victims); Credit Card Insurance (2.1 million victims); Unauthorized Billing—Internet Services (1.8 million victims); Advance-Fee Loans (1.7 million victims); Credit Repair Scams (1.2 million victims); and Business Opportunities (.8 million victims).[341]

In the United States, figures from all types of fraud indicated that, 20 percent of the victims are African Americans, 18 percent are Hispanics, 12 percent are Caucasians, and "in addition, the survey found that younger consumers, those who did not complete college and those with high levels of debt were more likely to be victims of fraud. Consumers between 65 and 74 years of age were 32 percent less likely to report having experienced fraud than those between 35 and 44."[342] These figures are for consumer fraud in general and differ from 419 scams specifically.

One of the most famous victims of the 419 scam is the former Iowa Congressman, Ed Mezvinsky, who was reported to have traveled to Nigeria several times and lost more than $3 million to 419 scammers.[343] It was reported that Mezvinsky was involved in more than three "black money" scams.[344] This contrasts sharply with the case of Janella Spears, a registered nurse and a reverend, from Oregon, who can be described as a gullible victim. She was a victim of a $400,000 scam. She received an e-mail from the 419 scammers telling her that her long lost grandfather left behind $20 million and that she needs to claim it.[345] It was reported that for two years she continued to send money to the scammers even after many people, including her family, friends, and law enforcement agents told her it is a scam.[346] She took money from her husband's retirement account, took out a lien on their car, and mortgaged their house and sent the money to the scammers.[347] It was reported that she carried on sending money to the scammers and she only stopped when investigators threatened to charge her with a crime.[348]

Another case worth mentioning is the scam involving Dr Louis A. Gottschalk. *The Los Angeles Times* of March 2, 2006, reported that Gottschalk, a University of California psychiatrist, lost at least $3 million to the Nigerian scam over a ten year period. This case also shows that there is no typical profile of 419 scam victims. Louis Gottschalk is a well-known neuroscientist whose impressive accomplishments include developing the Gottschalk-Gleser scales used in charting brain function impairments. He developed the scales with Goldine C. Gleser in 1969.
Dr. Louis Gottschalk traveled to Africa where he met the scammers. This scam was uncovered in a suit filed by his son, Dr. Guy Gottschalk, in February 2006 at the Orange County Superior Court. In the suit, Guy Gottschalk asked the court to remove his father as the administrator of their $8 million family partnership. Guy Gottschalk stated that his father must have been scammed of at least $3 million.[349] On the one hand, Guy Gottschalk maintained that the law suit will help stop his father from dealing with the 419 scammers. On the other hand, the attorney for Louis argued that Guy Gottschalk filed the law suit as a vendetta against his father. It was reported that Louis began sending money to the scammers as far back as 1995. It should be noted that an earlier suit filed by Guy Gottschalk to have a conservator oversee the family partnership was denied by the court. The court believed that Louis was competent to be an administrator of the partnership. It should be noted that Dr. Louis A.

Gottschalk passed away on November 27, 2008 at the age of 92.

Thomas A. Katona, former Alcona County Treasurer was also a victim of the Nigerian scam. He was caught up in the scam that he embezzled more than $1.2 million county funds through.[350] It was while Katona was on vacation in London that Alcona County treasury officers found out that he had made eight wire transfers of about $186,500 to overseas accounts.[351] Katona was arrested in November 2006 for embezzlement of county funds. Police investigations revealed that Katona sent $72,500 of his own money to the scammers in June 2006.[352] Katona was warned by bank officials, and some county employees about the 419 scam, but he ignored them.[353] There was enough evidence to charge Katona with embezzlement of county funds, and on January 17, 2007 he was charged with eight counts of embezzlement by a public official, which carries a 10-year maximum sentence if convicted, and one count of attempted embezzlement by a public official, which carries a five-year maximum sentence. Katona was also charged with two counts of forgery, which carries a 14-year maximum sentence if convicted.[354] In Alcona County, Michigan, Katona pleaded not guilty to the charges. Katona was found guilty. On June 12, 2007, Judge William F. Myles of the 23rd Circuit Court for the County of Alcona sentenced Katona to "6-10 years on eight counts of embezzlement by a public official over $50, 3-5 years on one count of attempted embezzlement by a public official over $50, and 9-14 years on two counts of forgery."[355]

Based on the amount of money that individuals give out to the scammers and also the fact that some of the victims travel to another country to meet the scammers, one can safely say that the majority of the international 419 victims are likely to be highly privileged members of society. Advance fee fraud, for instance, appears to be a middle class and upper class phenomenon. However, this claim merits further research. A study by the National Association of Securities Dealers found that individuals who fall within the high income bracket and who have financial education are most likely to be victims of money scams.[356] Another study also indicated that "high-achieving professionals are frequently defrauded, contrary to the widely held belief that the poorly educated and financially desperate are most vulnerable."[357]

> The research, carried out by Ultrascan, an IT fraud agency based in the Netherlands, also showed a strong correlation between white-collar victims and a recent or life-changing family trauma, which appeared to have impaired judgment. The review of 362 of the most serious cases, in which victims lost more than 150,000 British pounds, found that 85 percent had suffered a parent-related trauma – either death or an acrimous separation. The report concludes that those who have suffered bereavement appear to be more likely to be duped.[358]

It has also been noted that medical doctors are most likely to fall for these scams because they assume that the request for help is genuine and going to help the less privileged members of society.[359] Psychiatrists, psychologists, neuro-surgeons, and other specialists tend to be victims in a significant number of high-loss scams.[360] In a study involving 382 e-mail scam victims, 308 of the victims claimed that they had suffered child-parent trauma.[361] These victims included two police commissioners, 17 directors of companies, and entrepreneurs.[362]

As mentioned earlier, this scam is carried out mainly by Nigerians, both inside and outside Nigeria. Outside Nigeria, the countries with the highest number of 419 scammers operating within them are the United States, United Kingdom, The Netherlands, Greece, Malaysia, Romania, China, India, Spain and Italy.[363] Most 419 scam bank transfers involve Greek banks and it is estimated that at least 290 bank accounts in Greece have been used for these illicit bank payments.[364] It should be noted that most

419 scammers are likely to set up money transfers or money exchange agencies under which they carry out their scams, especially in Canada.[365] The countries with the biggest 419 scam losses are the United States, followed by the United Kingdom, and Japan.[366] Billions of dollars have been lost.[367]

4.7 THE WARNING SIGNS OF 419 SCAMS

The following are some of the warning signs of typical 419 scams. This list is not exhaustive and people should bear in mind that the scammers are constantly changing their method of operations.

1. Some of the scam letters are written entirely in capital letters. Note that it is unusual for genuine government and business officials to write a business letter all in capital letters.
2. The scam letters usually contain foreign telephone numbers and addresses. A website address is normally included in the letter. More often than not, there are two email addresses on the same letter. One is usually where the email was sent from and one at the bottom of the letter where you are told to send all correspondence.
3. The scam letters typically contain wrong spellings, bad grammar, combining small letters with capital letters indiscriminately. Note that all of these are done purposely by the scammers. This is part of the ploy to deceive you into thinking that they are real and do not know much. Do not fall for these.
4. The letters are marked as very urgent, confidential, and usually ask you to maintain secrecy at all times.
5. Personal identifying information is requested, including bank details. There may also be a request to send blank letterheads and invoices.
6. You will be asked to pay fees for several services, including the delivery of ATM cards, and fees for processing the transaction.

7. The name of the sender is different from the name of the person you are told to contact. Again, this is a deliberate ploy to deceive you.
8. You may be asked to travel to Nigeria or another country to complete the transaction.
9. The scammers usually claim to be top government officials, top military officials, lawyers, spouses or children of former government officials.
10. You are told you will receive a check, advised to deposit/cash it and send some percentage back to them. Do not get involved in this sort of thing. It is a warning sign. Legitimate businesses do not do this sort of thing.

4.8 CAN THE UNITED STATES STOP THIS SCAM?

Many Americans have fallen victim to the 419 scam, and this raises the question of why the United States cannot stop this scam. One key reason why the United States has not been able to stop this crime is because the 419 scam is a cybercrime. It is carried out mainly through the internet. The anonymity offered by the internet makes it difficult to stop the scam. The scammers do not use their real names, and in Nigeria there is no requirement or incentive for people to carry a state or national identity card, as we have in the United States.

Another reason why the United States has not been able to stop the 419 scam is because it is a transnational organized crime. This makes the investigation and prosecution problematic and in fact very expensive. There are jurisdictional issues involved, for instance. In fact, it has been observed that criminals choose to commit cybercrime more than the traditional forms of crime because the risk of conviction for cybercrimes is low.[368] The 419 scammers use e-mails to conduct their operations because the interception of e-mails by law enforcement agents is harder.[369]

The United States Secret Service is the agency responsible for financial crimes, including the 419 scam. However, they are assisted by other law enforcement agencies including the FBI and Interpol. Various initiatives have been put in place by the U.S. government to help stop this scam, but the scam still continues. In 1998, attempts were made to introduce a bill titled "The Nigerian Advance Fee Fraud Prevention Bill" in the U.S. Congress. The bill was not passed into law. It has been noted, however, that:

> Even if the Bill was to be enacted into law its success, if any, was bound to be circumscribed by the following limitations: first, there was nothing in the draft Bill that expressly penalized U.S. residents who agreed to illicit a money transfer from Nigeria for rewards under the obviously irregular circumstances that characterize advance fee fraud methodology. It is no less a crime to solicit help for the transfer of illicit money out of Nigeria for reward, than in acquiescing to such a criminal proposition. If the transaction were genuine, it would violate money laundering regulations. A specific law that criminalizes such a conspiracy in the U.S. would have much deterrent effect on advance fee fraud schemes targeted at U.S. residents, by effectively discouraging U.S. residents from responding to such solicitations.[370]

Taiwo Oriola maintained that it's impossible for the U.S. Congress to directly regulate a crime that originates from Nigeria, though he noted that "the absence of an advance fee fraud-specific legislation in the U.S. does not mean that the crime is beyond the remit of U.S. prosecutors. They could, for instance, make recourse to section 1341 of the Mail Fraud Act in prosecution of advance fee fraud related cases."[371]

Another reason why the United States has not been able to stop the 419 scam relates to the unwillingness of the Nigerian government to cooperate fully. Two reasons provide possible explanation for this. First, and as mentioned earlier, many of the Nigerian government officials are corrupt and are actually involved in the scam. Second, and according to the FBI, "The Nigerian government is not sympathetic to victims of these schemes, since the victim actually conspires to remove funds from Nigeria in a manner that is contrary to Nigerian law. The schemes themselves violate section 419 of the Nigerian criminal code, hence the label "419 fraud."[372]

4.9 PROSECUTIONS

There have been several prosecutions by the United States, the Nigerian government and other countries. On March 24, 2010, for instance, the United States Department of Justice announced in a press release that a Nigerian 419 scammer, Ugochukwu Enwerem, has been convicted of advance fee fraud.[373] Records indicated that from September 2002 and April 2007 Ugochukwu Enwerem, Kent Okogie, and others scammed at least 18 people in The United States and other countries and received at least $9.5 million.[374] This was mainly through the foreign lottery scam and the inheritance/next of kin scam.

Enwerem was convicted on one count of conspiracy to commit mail and wire fraud, and 14 counts of wire fraud. It should be noted that both individuals were extradited from the Netherlands to the United States. On February 23, 2011, Ugochukwu Enwerem was sentenced to 108 months in prison, ordered to serve three years of supervised release following the prison term. Judge Graham C. Mullen also ordered the forfeiture of $9,453,815,[375] and ordered Enwerem "to pay restitution in the same amount, jointly and severally with co-defendant Kent Okogie."[376] Kent Oserumen Okogie had earlier in November 2010 been sentenced to 72 months in prison.[377]

The largest 419 scam loss in history is the $242 million scam involving three Nigerians who were convicted of scamming Mr. Nelson Sakaguchi, the head of International Finance at Banco Noroeste in Sao Paolo, Brazil. This fraud led to the collapse of the bank. The scammers are

Emmanuel Nwude (former director of Union Bank Plc), Nzeribe Edeh Okolo, Mrs. Martina Amaka Anajemba. Their companies are Emrus (Nig) Ltd, Ocean Marketing Co. (Nig) Ltd., African Shelter Bureau (Nig) Ltd, and Finbaz, Nig, Ltd. It was reported that they convinced Mr. Nelson Sakaguchi into making several bank transfers between 1996 and 1998 into several bank accounts and promised him that he will personally receive $10 million for investing in a fictitious airport contract in Nigeria.[378] Sakaguchi made 8 installment payments to the scammers between 1995 and 1998.[379]

The Nigerian Economic and Financial Crimes Commission (EFCC), charged them with stealing and conspiracy under Sections 8(a) and 1(b) of the Advance Fee Fraud and other Related Offences Act 13 of 1995 as amended by Act 62 of 1999. The trial began in 2004. On July 16, 2005, Mrs. Anajemba pleaded guilty and was sentenced to two and a half years imprisonment. She also forfeited about N32 billion (Nigerian currency– Naira) in cash and assets. They were convicted at Ikeja High Court, Lagos. Justice Joseph Olubunmi Oyewole was the trial judge. Delivering the judgment, Justice Oyewole stated that "a balance must be arrived at by the court in ensuring that not only is the financial element, which induces and motivates this class of offenses taking care of but also imposes sanctions that would sign post to society that crime does not pay and that certain conduct is simply not acceptable."[380] The judge also stated that, "it is sad that the activities of the accused persons not only led to the collapse of a bank in a foreign country but also brought miseries to many innocent people."[381] Nwude was sentenced to 25 years in prison, ordered to forfeit $110 million to the bank, forfeit all his assets (property, shares, money, and cars) to the victims, his company also ordered to forfeit $11.5 million to the Nigerian Government.[382] Okolo was sentenced to 12 years in prison and forfeited his assets. So far, the EFCC has returned $17 million to Banco Noroeste.

4.10 WHAT IS TO BE DONE?

The 419 scams have severely affected the Nigerian image and the country's economy. One of the main economic effects is that the scams have led to less direct foreign investments in Nigeria. The Economic and Financial Crimes Commission (EFCC) is the Nigerian agency that deals with 419 scams. They collaborate with other local law enforcement agencies and foreign government agencies. The EFCC was established in 2004 under the EFCC Establishment Act of 2004.

The 419 scam is increasingly being carried out through the internet. Hence, one of the ways that governments can control the internet is through the intermediaries.[383] Internet Service Providers can be the best "gatekeepers" of the internet.[384] Therefore, governments can control internet users by controlling the internet service providers.[385] The idea of the government controlling the internet through the ISPs has been shown to be effective in Saudi Arabia, and even in China.[386]

Lawrence Lessig examined the claim that the present architecture of the Net makes it difficult for the government to regulate the architecture of the Net.[387] He noted that it is difficult for the government to regulate directly, and "so government regulates behavior indirectly by regulating architectures, which in turn influence or constrain behavior differently. This indirect regulation, at times quite effective, suggests a way of thinking about the example that started us down the road—certification."[388] Lessig believed that identification is very important and argued in favor of Internet Identity Card. I am also in support of a digital identity card, which we believe will help solve or at least minimize the anonymity on the internet, which makes cybercrime, especially the 419 scam continue to thrive. Internet Service Providers need to be given more roles and held liable for most of the internet abuses. Lessig, however, noted the fact that many people might revolt against the digital identity card program and he wrote:

> But it does not follow that government cannot create incentives for people to adopt identification technologies, even without directly

> mandating them. There is no requirement that all citizens have a driver's license, but you would find it very hard to get around without one, even if you do not drive. The government does not require that you keep state-issued identification on your persons, but if you want to fly to another city, you must show at least one form of such identification. The lesson is simple: make the incentive to carry ID so strong that no government requirement is necessary.[389]

Lessig also appeared to favor the government control of intermediaries when he wrote: "In the same way, the government could create incentives to enable digital IDs, not by regulating individuals directly but by regulating intermediaries. Intermediaries are fewer, their interests are usually commercial, and they are ordinarily pliant targets of regulation."[390] The various ways by which the government can create incentives for citizens to have digital IDs have been clearly outlined by Lessig.[391]

The 419 scam creates enormous financial and emotional burden on many people. After a critical analysis of some of the 419 letters, the modus operandi of the scammers and the socio-economic background of some of the victims, it is submitted that some of the victims should be charged with a crime. Some of these victims can be charged with crimes such as money laundering, violation of the United States Code on interstate transportation of wagering paraphernalia, and wire and mail fraud. As mentioned earlier, there is a high degree of criminal intent on the part of the victims in almost all the 419 scam letters examined for this book. Prosecuting some of the victims will serve as a deterrent for others considering getting involved in these illicit deals. There is no gainsaying the fact that greed plays a significant role in an individual's decision to respond to the 419 solicitations. Is it not a warning sign when somebody receives a letter from somebody he or she does not know asking that the person assist in getting money out of another country? This is a red flag. Moreover, most of the 419 scam correspondences ask the potential victim to lie and also to maintain secrecy in all the dealings. This is also a red flag. In fact, most of the 419 letters make it explicit that the deal is illegal.

4.11 CONCLUSION

The idea put forward by some scholars that Internet Service Providers should be held more accountable for the misuse of email accounts is a viable one. Similarly, the use of digital identity cards is necessary and hereby supported. There is also the need to ensure that people are made fully aware of the fact that under no circumstance should they respond to these scams and that failure to do so may result in criminal prosecution. Law enforcement agencies need to play more roles in educating and disseminating information to the public on these scams. Many people do not know that participation in foreign lottery is a federal crime, for instance. Governments need to embark on visible public relations campaigns aimed at warning people about these scams. Internet access is not available in many homes in Nigeria at the moment. The 419 scam is mainly carried out from the net cafes in the cities. Therefore, attempts to stop this scam must involve targeting and prosecuting the net cafes, as well as the internet service providers. In the final analysis, one can safely say that most 419 scam victims are to be blamed. There were warning signs throughout the process, but because of greed they fell into the trap.

It has been noted that the current collaboration among the different law enforcement agencies involved in the investigation and prosecution of these scams in various countries is inadequate.[392] Therefore, there should be international collaboration based on uniform treaties and laws.[393] In a nutshell, there are two main ways of tackling the 419 scams—deterrence and prosecution. Deterring the general public involves educating them about the dynamics, and consequences of involvement in these scams.

CHAPTER 5
COMBATING TERRORISM

5.1 INTRODUCTION

After the September 11, 2001 terrorist attacks in the United States, efforts to combat terrorism intensified. Several organizations, governments, and scholars from various backgrounds put forward several recommendations on how to combat terrorism. This chapter presents an easy to understand examination of the strategies for combating terrorism and for stopping and containing the fundamentalist ideologies that are fueling and supporting terrorism.

5.2 WHAT IS TERRORISM?

Terrorism is the deliberate use of different forms of extreme violence against human beings and property by an individual or group of individuals, aimed at influencing social, economic and political systems. Terrorism is a crime. Therefore, terrorists are criminals. One of the aims of terrorists is to instill fear in people and disrupt normal activities. Terrorism is a complex and multivariate phenomenon, made up of different forms, and occurs in different parts of the world, with different objectives.[394] No type of political system is immune from terrorism. In recent times, however, most terrorist acts have been directed at the United States and other Western, liberal, democratic states and their allies. Terrorist acts can be carried out by individuals from different religious backgrounds.

Terrorism can be classified into domestic or international. Domestic terrorism may be defined as terrorist acts committed within a particular state by an individual or group of individuals within that state without direct foreign support.[395] According to the FBI:

> International terrorism involves violent acts or acts dangerous to human life that are a violation of the criminal laws of the United States or any state, or that would be a criminal violation if committed within the jurisdiction of the United States or any state. These acts appear to be intended to intimidate or coerce a civilian population, influence the policy of a government by intimidation or coercion, or affect the conduct of a government by assassination or kidnapping. International terrorist acts occur outside the United States or transcend national boundaries in terms of the means by which they are accomplished, the persons they appear intended to coerce or intimidate, or the locale in which their perpetrators operate or seek asylum.[396]

5.3 CAUSES OF TERRORISM

Terrorism can take many forms, and terrorists have different motives and come from different ideological and religious backgrounds. Hence, there is no "one-size-fits-all explanation" for terroristic behavior.[397] It has been noted that:

> The process of becoming a terrorist involves a cumulative, incrementally sustained, and focused commitment to the group. For the majority of contemporary terrorists – whether religious or secular – there is an early entrance onto the pathway into terrorism with many stages along the way. Also, as we have seen, there is a continuing reinforcement by manipulative leaders by consolidating the collective identity and by externalizing, justifying, and requiring violence against the enemy. This implies that early intervention is required, for once a youth is embedded within the group his or her extremist psychology is continually reinforced and any doubts diminished.[398]

Terrorists can be males or females, and they have various methods of operation. Hence, many things can cause terrorism. Over the years, scholars have struggled with coming up with acceptable causes of terrorism. However, there are psychological, biological, political, economic, as well as social/environmental explanations of terrorism. Recently, there have been several studies linking poverty, education, and globalization with terrorism. Terrorists may not be abnormal, but terrorism itself is an abnormal activity.[399] Terrorism involves extremely violent acts; terrorists tend to live stressful and isolated lives, and all of these make us wonder why and how some people end up becoming terrorists.[400] Put simply,

> Terrorists are generally people who feel alienated from society and have a grievance or regard themselves as victims of an injustice. Many are dropouts. They are devoted to their political or religious cause and do not regard their violent actions as criminal. They are loyal to each other but will deal with a disloyal member more harshly than the enemy. They are people with cunning skill, and initiative, as well as ruthlessness. In order to be initiated into the group, the new recruit may be expected to perform an armed robbery or murder. They show no fear, pity, or remorse. The sophistication of the terrorist will vary depending on the significance and context of the terrorist action. The Colombian hostage-takers who infiltrated an embassy party and the Palace of Justice, for example, were far more sophisticated than would be, for example, Punjab terrorists who gun down bus passengers. Terrorists have the ability to use a variety of weapons, vehicles, and communications equipment and are familiar with their physical environment, whether it be a 747 jumbo jet or a national courthouse. A terrorist will rarely operate by himself/herself or

> in groups, unless the operation requires taking over a large building, for example.[401]

Psychological Explanations

Why do "normal-looking" people decide to engage in aberrant behavior, such as terrorism? Are terrorists psychologically abnormal? Are they mentally ill? Psychologists, psychiatrists, and criminologists have tried to answer these questions and the majority of them believe that terrorists are psychologically normal people. Audrey Cronin maintained that certain childhood events and peer pressure are two of the reasons why some people join a group, arguing that, "the individual's psychological make-up alone rarely is sufficient explanation for involvement in terrorist activities. On average, terrorists are no more "crazy" than the rest of humanity."[402]

Jerrold Post also examined the psychological basis of terrorists and terrorism and concluded that terrorists are psychologically normal individuals.[403] Terrorists are not depressed individuals; they are not severely emotionally disturbed; revenge seems to be one of the motivations for some terrorists, for some other terrorists, terrorism gives "a sense of power to the powerless; for still others, it is to gain a sense of significance."[404]

It has been recognized that in order to inhibit people from falling into this violent path, that early interventions are necessary.[405] Such interventions include countering the message of hatred of the terrorist groups, and getting the media, educational, religious, and social organizations involved, as well as providing avenues for integration.[406] John Horgan contended that:

> Psychopathic behavior and many features of terrorist violence have similarities, notably in terms of how terrorists respond to their victims: if terrorists perpetuate violence often resulting in the death of non-combatants then surely they must lack empathy or remorse; this is reinforced given their antisocial and irresponsible behavior, and even more so when

> the terrorists, not content with destruction in itself, subsequently claims responsibility for the act. The tendency to ascribe explanations of outright abnormality/mental illness owing to the savagery of the behavior is noted by many, and even go as far as to suggest sadism. Empirical evidence or not such explanations pass for plausible.[407]

Some scholars believe that terrorists are genuinely mad. Walter Laqueur for instance, argued that "madness, especially paranoia, plays a role in contemporary terrorism. Not all paranoiacs are terrorists, but all terrorists believe in conspiracies by the powerful, hostile forces and suffer from some form of delusion and persecution mania. The element of madness plays an important role, even if many are reluctant to acknowledge it."[408] For me, most terrorists are psychologically normal people who are acting out their deep-rooted dissatisfactions with social, economic, and political systems. However, some terrorists have been known to exhibit some forms of psychopathic behavior. This on its own does not cause terrorism. Other factors, such as the social environment, play a crucial role. There are no clearly defined terrorist personality characteristics at the moment. In fact and as Horgan has pointed out, "The rigor of research pointing to either explicit or implicit abnormality, or to the existence of a 'terrorist personality' is such that its propositions are built on unsteady empirical, theoretical and conceptual foundations."[409]

Biological Explanations

Are there biological explanations for terrorism? There is no scientific research showing any biological explanation as to why some people become terrorists. In fact, there is no evidence at the moment to suggest any genetic role in the determination of who may or not become a terrorist.[410] However, Andrew Silke contended that age and gender are the key biological factors related to terrorist group membership, arguing that "while a causative role for these factors is not entirely unambiguous, there is certainly a correlation between the two factors and most recruits to terrorist organizations. Most people who join a terrorist group are young, and by young here we are referring to teenagers and people in their early twenties, and most new recruits are male."[411] This view is supported by criminological theories. In fact, several research studies on violent crime throughout the world have shown that violent crime offenders tend to be males between the ages of 15 and 25.[412] Silke studied 89 loyalist paramilitaries in Northern Ireland, and found that the youngest members carried out most of the bombings and assassinations and that "the median age of these individuals was 23 years old, compared to a median of 28 years for those involved with the low-risk vigilante activities of the group, and a median age of 39 for those involved in the very low-risk fundraising operations."[413] In a list containing the names of terrorists wanted by the Saudi Interior Ministry, 23 of the 35 people on the list were aged between 21 and 25 years. The oldest person in the list was aged 40 years.[414] As we can see from the above and from other research studies, there is what can be safely called the "age of criminality."

Social Identification and Marginalization (Environmental Factors)

Social identification and marginalization may lead to terrorism. Here we are talking about the social environment that may be breeding terrorism or gives rise to terrorists. Hence, any attempt to understand why some people become terrorists must also involve an attempt at understanding the psychology of vengeance.[415] As one commentator has pointed out, "one important element of the desire for vengeance is the surprising willingness of individuals to sacrifice and suffer in order to carry out an act of vengeance."[416] The most convincing explanation of what causes terrorism is the social and environmental factors. Those who feel humiliated and marginalized will more often than not engage in conflicts. James Gilligan has pointed out:

> I have yet to see a series of violence that was not provoked by the experience of feeling shamed and humiliated, disrespected and ridiculed, and that did not represent the

> attempt to prevent or undo this 'loss of face' - no matter how severe the punishment, even if it includes death. For we misunderstand these men, at our peril, if we do not realize they mean it literally when they say they would rather kill or mutilate others, be killed or mutilated themselves, than live without pride, dignity and self-respect.[417]

Most terrorists usually report using terrorism as a tool for revenge. Hence, it is no surprise that the examination of personal histories of terrorists "frequently contain encounters with members of the security forces or rival groups where the individual, friends or family members were threatened, harassed, assaulted or even killed, and such catalyst events leave the potential terrorists (usually teenagers or in their early twenties at the time) with a powerful desire for vengeance."[418] In fact, it has been noted that joining a terrorist group in the aftermath of acts of violence against one's self, loved ones, or others they strongly identify with, is a common theme for more ideological terrorist groups.[419]

5.4 BACKGROUND OF SOME TERRORISTS

In the previous section we discussed the causes of terrorism. In this section, we examine the socio-economic and political backgrounds of some known terrorists. On March 11, 2004, terrorists struck in Madrid, Spain. Ten bombs exploded in four crowded commuter trains during rush hour. About 191 people died and more than 1,800 were injured. Three other bombs failed to explode. **Jamal Ahmidan** was one of the terrorists who carried out the attacks. He was from Morocco, aged 34, and an undocumented immigrant living in Spain at the time. Ahmidan had a past history of criminality. He spent time in prison for his involvement in a series of petty crimes. He was also convicted in Morocco in 2000 for murder. It was reported that after his release from prison, he began to attend the mosque regularly and became an extremist. Ahmidan was one of the seven terrorists who blew themselves up when the police went to arrest them. He was a drug dealer known as "the Chinaman." It was reported that it was the money from his drug deals that financed the terrorist attacks, especially the purchase of the dynamites used in the attacks.[420] **Othman el-Gnaoui** was another terrorist involved in the 2004 Madrid attacks. He was aged 32, and seen to be Ahmidan's most-trusted assistant. On October 31, 2007, he was also convicted of the Madrid terrorist attacks. He also had past involvement in crimes. In fact, before the Madrid attacks, he was already under police surveillance for drug deals. He also blew himself up when police closed in on them. **Asrih Rifaat Anwar,** aged 24, Moroccan, was also involved in the Madrid attacks and also blew himself up when the police closed in on them. He also had a previous criminal record, having been arrested for drug possession and dealing. **Abdennabi Kounjaa**, aged 29, Moroccan, was also found guilty of the Madrid attacks. His prior arrests before the Madrid bombings were for car theft and for smuggling. He used to be a teacher at a local mosque. **Rachid Oulad Akcha,** aged 33, Moroccan, a student at the time of the attack, was also involved in the Madrid attacks. He also blew himself up when the police surrounded their apartment. He also has a history of past criminality, having been convicted of drug trafficking.

Other terrorists convicted of the Madrid terrorist bomb attacks include **Jamal Zougan,** Moroccan, believed to have close links with Al-Qaeda leadership; **Allekema Lamari**, Algerian; **Sarhane Ben Abdelmajid Fakhet**, Tunisian; and **Rabei Osman**, among others. It was reported that about 28 people were involved in the attacks. Unfortunately, we do not have records on whether all of them had prior involvement in criminality. However, from the information below, one can safely draw a conclusion that they all had past involvement in many types of crime. *The Guardian* of October, 31, 2007, reported that the Madrid terrorist bomb cell;

> was larger, much more experienced, more closely connected to Al-Qaeda or at least to European Islamist organizations linked to Al-

> Qaeda, radicalized over a longer period of time, extensively involved in criminal activities, and less assimilated. None of the members was a Spanish citizen; most were Moroccan. They were linked together through several different connections, primarily family and prison experience. Some members of the group frequented a mosque in the Tetan quarter of Madrid, but religious institutions were apparently not the critical factor—in fact, the conspirators rejected some mosques as insufficiently radical. They met in mundane locations – restaurants, hairdressers' establishments, phone booths, and private apartments. The network of associations was particularly dense and large.[421]

The Madrid terrorist bomb attacks discussed above contrasts sharply with the July 7, 2005 terrorist attacks in London, where the perpetrators had no officially recorded history of crime. In fact, the key difference between the two attacks is that the London attackers were homegrown terrorists while the Madrid attackers were foreigners. On July 7, 2005, a series of bombs exploded on London's public transport system—commuter trains and buses. Around 8:30 a.m. three bombs exploded within seconds of each other at three different underground train stations, and a fourth bomb exploded at Tavistock Square at 9:47 a.m.. A total of 52 people died, four of the suicide bombers also died, and about 700 were injured. Three of the four main suspects were British-born citizens with Pakistani origin and they had no police records. The suspects were: **Mohammed Siddique Khan**, aged 30, believed to be a heavy user of cannabis and a heavy drinker, before he became a devout Muslim in 2000. Khan was a counselor at a center for children with disabilities. The second terrorist was **Shahzad Tanweer**, aged 22, who was responsible for the bomb that exploded at Aldgate Train Station. **Hasib Hussain,** aged 19 was the third terrorist who was responsible for the bomb that killed 13 people on a double-decker bus. **Jermaine Lindsay** was the fourth terrorist in this attack.

Commenting on what motivates these homegrown terrorists, Zachary Coile stated that "young Muslims who are drawn to extremist groups are often angry over global events, especially the Palestinian-Israeli conflict and the war in Iraq, but also feel a sense of social alienation at home in the West. Radical groups prey on these emotions when recruiting on the Internet chat rooms and at universities and Islamic bookstores."[422] It appears that homegrown terrorists do not usually have any documented past police records of criminality. In fact, five of the six men arrested in the United States in June 2006, in connection with the plot to blow up Chicago's Sears Tower and other buildings were homegrown terrorists, with no prior police records. Those charged with that terrorist plot are: **Patrick Abraham, Burson Augustin**, **Rothschild Augustine**, **Narseal Batiste**, **Lyglensen Lemorin**, **Naudimar Herrera,** and **Stanley Grant Phanor**. This emerging pattern of homegrown terrorists is a grave concern to law enforcement agents. Cultural alienation, the influence of radical clerics and even youthful rebellion are some of the motivations for these terrorist activities.[423] FBI director, Robert Mueller has also expressed serious concern about this new group of homegrown terrorists. He noted that "these homegrown terrorists may prove to be as dangerous as groups like Al-Qaeda, if not more so."[424] These homegrown terrorists tend to be self-recruited, self-trained, self-executing, operate through the internet, and are inspired by radical websites that call for violence.[425]

Another act of terrorism worth mentioning is the terrorist attack that happened in Ankara, Turkey, in 2007. The lone suicide bomber—**Guven Akkus,** aged 28, carried out a suicide attack that killed six people. A total of 91 people were injured. The suicide attack took place at a bus stop in front of Anfartalar Shopping Mall in May 2007. Akkus had past history of criminality, including a conviction for hanging illegal posters, and resisting arrest. He served two years in prison for this particular offense. It is not clear if he had any links with the Kurdistan Workers Party (PKK), but what we do know is that the equipment and explosives that he used in the attack were the same as those normally used by the PKK.

In Moscow, on October 23, 2002, 50 terrorists stormed into a Moscow theater and held 700 people hostage. They demanded that Russia withdraw her forces immediately from Chechnya. Hence, many people believed that these terrorists were acting in retaliation of Russia's brutality against Chechnya, but these terrorists were actually radicalized criminals before the 1999 invasion.[426] The architect of this hostage was **Movsar Baraev**, aged 22, a citizen of Chechnya. He is a known gang member, who comes from a gang family that was involved in many types of crime including kidnappings. It was reported that Baraev became the leader of his uncle's gang after his uncle was killed in 2001. There are reports that, "Movsar Baraev inherited more than his uncle's position as a criminal gang leader; he also inherited his ties to the world of global terrorism. Russian forces had identified Movsar as a conduit for funds from foreign terrorist organizations, and had targeted him for destruction a year ago."[427]

Velupillai Prabhakaran was one of the leaders of Liberation Tigers of TAMIL Eelam (LTTE). He was born on November 27, 1954. His father was a Hindu government official. Prabhakaran was a gang member, and dropped out of school at age 16. He was involved in kidnappings and killings. Prabhakaran is one of the people accused of murdering Rajiv Gandhi.

Abu Nidal, born with the name Sabri al-Banna in May of 1937 in Jaffa, Palestine. He was the leader of the Abu Nidal Organization (ANO). His father was one of the wealthiest property dealers. In 1948, three years after his father's death, however, his family went into extreme poverty. The Israeli government confiscated their lands.[428] The confiscation of their land by the Israeli government could imply that they were involved in some form of illegal activities/criminality. He was arrested by the Egyptian authorities in 1998 for carrying a Tunisian passport with a false name.[429] He was a member of the Ba'ath Party. He did not complete his engineering program at Cairo University. It is believed that Nidal suffered from paranoid psychopathology.[430]

Osama bin Laden, head of Al-Qaeda, born Usama bin Muhammad bin Laden on July 30, 1957, in Riyadh, Saudi Arabia. His father was the wealthiest building construction contractor in Saudi Arabia. He studied management and economics at King Abdul Aziz University in Jeddah. He is believed to be responsible for the 9/11 attacks. There is no official record showing that he had past history of criminality. Based on his socio-economic background, it is most likely that he had no prior criminal records before he became involved in terrorism. Osama bin Laden was killed by the United States Navy Seals on July 1, 2011 at his hideout in Abbottabad in Pakistan.

5.5 PAST CRIMINALITY AND TERRORIST POTENTIAL

Having examined the backgrounds of some terrorists, we now examine the issue of whether there is a link between past criminality and terrorist potential. . Why do we think that there is a link? Several theories and studies point to this. A study by Yvon Dandurand and Vivienne Chin, for instance, showed that:

> It is not particularly uncommon for terrorist groups to recruit some of their members among criminal elements, particularly among individuals who may have special skills or special access to networks or criminal opportunities. A terrorist organization can include common criminals who contribute to its goals in instrumental, training, and other manners (Amir, 1988). In such a group, part of the membership can actually be specializing in committing crime and there may be obvious reasons for these sub-groups to be kept quite isolated from the rest of the organization.[431]

Moreover, and as mentioned earlier, new recruits may be expected to commit robbery or murder before they are allowed to join a terrorist group. There is general agreement among criminologists that involvement in petty crimes may lead to future involvement in major crimes. In fact, it has been observed that the decrease in New York City's crime rate since 1990 has been as a result of "an aggressive policy toward deterring petty crime, which then leads to reduced levels of major crime."[432] There is also common belief among criminologists that "violent people are violent, in part, because they grow up in a milieu that lacks social controls through family and school, and are exposed to groups which encourage a code of violence, whether for crime or self-respect."[433] Cesare Lombroso, an Italian criminologist, in his theory of atavism, came up with the idea that there are occasional criminals and criminaloids.[434] The occasional criminals commit crime to protect family honor and as self-defense. Criminaloids commit crimes when the opportunities arise. This theory can be used to explain why most terrorists come from particular countries like Morocco and Afghanistan. The environment in these countries predisposes some of these individuals to engage in violent activities.

A report by Britain's M15 titled "Understanding Radicalisation and Violent Extremism in the UK," noted that "terrorist groups are remarkably tolerant of individuals with serious criminal histories. This is the case even when those individuals continue to be involved in very serious non-terrorist crimes, including drug-trafficking, assault and even rape."[435] According to the M15, some criminals are attracted to the violent aspects of terrorism.[436] Furthermore, a study by Lt. Col. Jon Drummond, titled "Who Will Be Violent?: Correlates of Overt Activism and Criminality Among U.S. White Separatists," found that of the 35 males and six females in his study, that 43.9 percent had some sort of prior involvement with the criminal justice system.[437] It is possible that there is a link between past criminality and terrorist potential. This contention deserves further studies. A large database containing the criminal history of convicted terrorists is needed. We also need more empirical studies to ascertain to what degree this link exists.

5.6 FUNDAMENTALIST IDEOLOGIES

Fundamentalist ideologies are all about hatred, violence, intolerance, and extreme interpretation of doctrines. There are many fundamentalist groups, and their ideologies can either be politically or religiously motivated. There are Islamic fundamentalists, Christian fundamentalists, and others. It should be noted that Jihad is an ideology that drives and motivates Islamic extremists. Fundamentalist groups use all means available to them. They use violence against other people and will even go as far as to sacrifice their own lives for their "cause." Ustaz Muhammed Bin Ali was right when he wrote that:

> Essentially, the extremist fail to understand the peaceful message of Islam, leading them to believe that, at the core, the relationship between Muslims and non-Muslims must be driven by enmity and hostility. Consequently, it solicits revulsion of anyone or anything that they perceive as infidel. The perception is craftily tweaked to advocate and legitimize unrelenting war and aggression, and to kill, all of which stem from the overwhelming and uncontrolled feelings of hatred.[438]

The characteristics of radical fundamentalists include: their open and aggressive hostility toward the United States, a goal of damaging and destroying democratic society, imposing and expanding the strict observance of Islam, often uncomfortable with modernity, and many of them lack education, even about the principles of their own religion, relying instead on superstitions and local tradition.[439] Al-Qaeda and Jemaah Islamiyah are examples. Jemaah Islamiyah is a terrorist organization based in Indonesia. It is affiliated to Al-Qaeda and has terror cells in Singapore, Malaysia, Australia, and the Philippines. Jemaah Islamiyah is anti-America and its Western allies, with the aim of establishing pan-Islamic caliphates.[440]

5.7 STRATEGIES FOR COMBATING TERRORISM, FOR STOPPING AND CONTAINING THE FUNDAMENTALIST IDEOLOGIES

It has been noted that terrorist groups rarely achieve their goals and that there are several ways through which terrorist groups end. Leonard Weinberg and Arie Perliger studied 232 terrorist groups and concluded that terrorist groups end by the capture or killing of group leadership (30.6 percent); repression by the authorities (21.9 percent); the group abandons terrorism in favor of non-violent tactics (12.5 percent); merger with another terrorist group (12.1 percent); group achieves its goals (7.7 percent); loss of public support (4.3 percent); internal ideological disputes and power struggles (3.4 percent); loss of state support (for groups that were state supported) (3.4 percent); failure to recruit a new generation (2.5 percent); and groups adopt other types of violence (1.2 percent).[441] They maintained that terrorist groups end through four main ways—external repression, internal collapse, public rejection and success.[442] Their study faced some criticism. Audrey Cronin for instance, argued that there are six pathways to how terrorist groups end—decapitation, negotiations, success, failure, repression and reorientation.[443] Cronin argued that “it is not clear how the 232 groups studied by Weinberg and Perliger were ‘coded’—for example, what guided decisions about which groups to label with which ending.”[444] The study was also criticized, because it did not include negotiation as one of the pathways through which terrorist groups end.[445]

Military force alone usually does not end terrorism. In fact, a study of 648 terrorist groups that existed between 1968 and 2006 showed that only seven percent of the terrorist groups ended through military force.[446] The study also found that 43 percent of the terrorist groups ended through transition into a political process.[447] It should be noted, however, that;

> The possibility of a political solution is inversely linked to the breadth of terrorist goals. Most terrorist groups that end because of politics

> seek narrow policy goals. The narrower the goals of a terrorist organization, the more likely it can achieve them without violent action—and the more likely the government and terrorist group may be able to reach a negotiated settlement.[448]

Military force is usually very effective when used against large, well-armed, and well-organized insurgent groups.[449] Religiously motivated terrorist groups are more problematic to contain and end for several reasons. These groups tend to seek unobtainable and illusive goals. An analysis of 648 terrorist groups by Seth G. Jones and Martin C. Libicki revealed that Al-Qaeda has close to zero percent chance of overthrowing a government.[450] No religiously motivated terrorist group ended by victory since 1968.[451] As Jones and Libicki have correctly pointed out, Al-Qaeda "has virtually unachievable objectives in trying to overthrow multiple regimes in the Middle East. To make matters worse, virtually all government across Europe, North America, South America, Asia, the Middle East, and Africa consider al Qaida and enemy."[452] The study of 648 terrorist groups by Jones and Libicki found that:

1. Religious terrorist groups take longer to eliminate than other groups. Approximately 62 percent of all terrorist groups have ended since 1968, but only 32 percent of religious terrorist groups have ended.
2. Religious groups rarely achieve their objectives. No religious group that has ended achieved victory since 1968.
3. Size is a significant determination of a group's fate. Big groups of more than 10,000 members have been victorious more than 25 percent of the time, while victory is rare when groups are smaller than 1,000 members.
4. There is no statistical correlation between the duration of a terrorist group and ideological motivation, economic conditions, regime type, or breadth of terrorist goals.

But, there appears to be some correlation between size of a terrorist group and duration: Larger groups tend to last longer than smaller groups.

5. When a terrorist group becomes involved in an insurgency, it does not end easily. Nearly 50 percent of the time groups ended by negotiating a settlement with the government; 25 percent of the time they achieved victory; and 19 percent of the time military forces defeated them.
6. Terrorist groups from upper-income countries are more likely to be left-wing or nationalist and much less likely to be motivated by religion.[453]

At this point, it should be noted that the United States has a national strategy for combating terrorism, which can be summarized in the following words:

> From the beginning, the War on Terror has been both a battle of arms and a battle of ideas —a fight against the terrorists and their murderous ideology. In the short run, the fight involves the application of all instruments of national power and influence to kill or capture the terrorists; deny them safe haven and control of any nation; prevent them from gaining access to WMD; render potential terrorist targets less attractive by strengthening security; and cut off their sources of funding and other resources they need to operate and survive. In the long run, winning the War on Terror means winning the battle of ideas. Ideas can transform the embittered and disillusioned either into murderers willing to kill innocents, or into free peoples living harmoniously in a diverse society.[454]

The United States National Strategy for Combating Terrorism (2006) states that in order to win the War on Terror, the United States will do the following: advance effective democracies as the long-term antidote to the ideology of terrorism, prevent attacks by terrorist networks, deny weapons of mass destruction to rogue states and terrorist allies who seek to use them, deny terrorists the support and sanctuary of rogue states, deny terrorists control of any nation they would use as a base and launching pad for terror, and lay the foundations and build the institutions and structures we need to carry the fight forward against terror and help ensure our ultimate success.[455]

The U.S. long-term approach for winning the War on Terror is the advancement of freedom and human dignity through effective democracy.[456] The U.S. government believes that "democracy is the antithesis of terrorist tyranny, which is why the terrorists denounce it and are willing to kill the innocent to stop it. Democracy is based on empowerment, while the terrorists' ideology is based on enslavement. Democracies expand the freedom of their citizens, while terrorists seek to impose a single set of narrow beliefs."[457] The U.S. short-term strategy is to prevent terrorist attacks, deny terrorists entry to the United States and disrupt their travel internationally, defend potential targets of attack, and deny weapons of mass destruction to rogue states and terrorist allies who seek to use them. After a critical examination of the current U.S. national strategy, one can safely say that the current U.S. long-term strategy for combating terrorism relies heavily on advancing democracy. In my view, education should be an antidote. The current strategy undervalues the role of education in all of these. Other scholars have also criticized the current U.S. national strategy for combating terrorism. In fact,

> The current U.S. National Security Strategy for fighting the war against terrorism is under attack as a policy that is unsustainable, unilateral and a marked departure from the past U.S. principles. It calls for an open-ended war against terrorism that continues to be costly to the United States both in blood and treasure. Although the doctrine calls for the promotion of democracy and human rights

> around the world, it is perceived as being largely words without action, and when action is called for, it is through force. To win the fight against terrorism an alternative strategy is needed. A strategy that is sustainable and can be supported at home and abroad – the strategy of containment. It is a strategy that succeeded in winning the Cold War and is capable of reclaiming America's once high international stature. It is a sensible policy that relies on diplomacy, economic incentives, respect for international institutions and stresses the importance of allies for its success. However, not all aspects of the strategy of containment implemented during the Cold War will transfer to today's war on terrorism.[458]

As some scholars have pointed out, terrorism tends to occur when opportunity, motivation, and capability exist.[459] Muhammad Haniff Bin Hassan maintained that in order to prevent terrorism, we need to eliminate at least one of the three elements, especially motivation, which is driven by an ideology.[460] It is easier to eliminate or reduce the opportunity and the capability, but not easy to eliminate ideology. This explains why current strategies have not been very successful. We have to counter the ideologies of fundamentalist groups. Hassan came up with three types of terrorists and the role of ideology. The first type is the *Political Strategist*. As the name suggests, this type of terrorist is politically driven and "strives for power so he can impose his will on society."[461] The second type is the *Radical Theorist*.

> The Radical Theorist is more interested in the ideas that he believes in, than any political goal including power. He will not compromise his beliefs for the sake of power. The Radical Theorist may not be involved directly in terrorist acts, but acts as ideologue for the terrorist organization. He develops and refines the belief system, and defends them from criticism. He is skilled in offering rational and religious

> justifications for the terrorists. To him, ideas are the ends, not the means.[462]

The third type of terrorist is the *Militant Activists,* who are "drawn to violence as an end in itself, either as a means of venting anger, or as a source of excitement and adventure. Even without any ideology, they will be doing what they want to anyway."[463] Arguably, this type is mainly teenagers and young men. And they are most likely to be the homegrown terrorists that we are seeing today in the United States and the United Kingdom. It should also be kept in mind that these militant activists may not be affiliated to any terrorist organizations. At best, they may be described as sympathizers. They share the same characteristics as fire setters (arsonists). Many of them get thrills from arson. They are most likely to live near the area of the criminal acts. These types of terrorists are easier to stop and contain through regular police work, community policing programs, and domestic counterterrorism units.

A counterterrorism ideological response, targeted primarily at the majority of Muslims, not the terrorists, has been suggested.[464] Hassan contended that,

> A comprehensive approach encompassing ideological response is necessary due to the fact that terrorism, like an insurgency, is rooted on various factors. In the case of Al-Qaeda, its inclination towards terrorism is not only because of the ideology but also fueled by the context that provides them with the justification of their misinterpretation of Islam. The context also contributes in motivating Muslims to embrace the ideology. In many statements, Al-Qaeda clearly strives to position itself as the champion for Muslims grievances, for example, in Kashmir under the rule of the predominantly Hindu India, the long oppression of Muslims in Chechnya by the atheist Russians, the suffering of the Palestinians at the hands of the Jews, the death of civilian Iraqis due to the economic blockade by the international community and

> the hypocrisy of the United States' foreign policies."[465] Hassan believed that the objectives of the counterterrorism ideological response should be to "immunize general Muslims from extremist ideology, persuade less fanatic members of terrorist groups to abandon the ideology, create doubt and dissension within terrorist organizations, rehabilitate detained terrorist members and to immunize non-Muslims' anxiety and suspicion by presenting alternatives to terrorist ideology.[466]

In a similar vein, Jonathan Dean maintained that we need to "blunt the appeal of terrorist ideology to its adherents and to potential new recruits."[467] How to do this and who should do it becomes the key issue. An organized and systematic campaign coordinated by an organized and civil society organization has been suggested.[468] The Weapons of Mass Destruction Commission should "advocate the establishment of a multinational non-governmental foundation with the explicit objective of developing methods and measures to undermine the authority and appeal of radical Islamist ideology promoting the use of force and violence."[469] It has been argued that the non-governmental foundation should be staffed mainly by Muslims.[470] In as much as I agree with this, there are doubts, however, as to how effective this will be. Will there be backlash? Will the staff be treated as traitors? These questions and many more need to be addressed.

There is now general belief and understanding that the war on terror cannot be won by military action alone. This has even been echoed by the top military officials. For instance, General David Petraeus has noted that the United States "cannot kill its way to victory." There is the need to blunt the fundamentalist ideologies. The current United States strategy has not solved the problems because of the over-reliance on democratization. The current strategy places more emphasis on disrupting terrorist plots and killing top terrorist leaders. These are short time strategies, and we need to balance them with a long term strategy of education. There is no gainsaying the fact, however, that the current U.S. strategy has had some success. In fact Al-Qaeda's leadership and strength has diminished as a result of the current strategy, to some extent.

It is my belief that education that includes the de-radicalization of terrorists and potential recruits is the key and crucial long-term solution for combating terrorism and for stopping and containing the fundamentalist ideologies that are fueling terrorism. This assertion can be supported by the work of Jessica Stern of Harvard Law School, who has addressed the question of whether it is possible to de-radicalize terrorists. Stern examined a pioneer rehabilitation effort by Saudi Arabia where, since 2004, 4,000 militants have gone through a rehabilitation program and "the graduates have been reintegrated into mainstream society much more successfully than ordinary criminals."[471] The program involved encouraging the militants (called beneficiaries) to abandon their radical ideology, renounce their violent means, or both. One of the most interesting things about this program is that reintegration assistance is provided, and there is follow-up surveillance. The program is prison-based, and involves religious reeducation, psychological counseling, job training and assistance, career counseling, and raising self-esteem. The Saudi government and many scholars see the Saudi Arabia program as a success. The recidivism rate has been put at 10 to 20 percent.[472] Other countries should adopt this type of rehabilitation program.

It is submitted that Imams should be held more accountable. They should be required to openly condemn and discredit the radical extremists. It is worrying that some of these Imams are allowed to preach their message of hatred and violence in Western countries. The question now is—-have we become victims of our own liberalism? In the final analysis, there is every indication that Al-Qaeda will eventually disintegrate and probably turn into just a political group. This conclusion is based on a critical examination of the various pathways through which terrorist groups end. Even the Levellers, a political movement in England, were eventually contained.

5.8 CONCLUSION

Terrorist attacks are like earthquakes. We do not know when they will happen, but what we do know is that they are likely to happen. Therefore, we have to prepare for them. Based on the evaluation of the background of the terrorists examined in this book and on available literature, one can safely say that there is a possible link between past criminality and terrorist potential. Political, criminological, and sociological theories support this claim. Because of the small number of terrorists in this book, it is not clear at this point the extent or degree to which this link exists. Further research is needed in this area.

My examination of the background of some of the leaders of terrorist groups did not reveal past history of criminality before they became terrorists. The link that exists relates mainly to the terrorist operatives and/or those who become suicide bombers. The non-criminal past of most of the terrorist leaders could be explained by the fact that most of them came from wealthy families and attained university education. This contrasts sharply with the suicide bombers who as the evidence in this book suggests, tend to have past history of crime. This book has also found out that the leaders of these groups do not become suicide bombers. The majority of the terrorists in this study had past history of crime. However, the homegrown terrorists examined in this study did not have any official record of past involvement in crime.

Criminal justice policies, national security policies, counterterrorism strategies and foreign policy strategies differ for various crimes, and for terrorism. Since there is a possible link between past criminality and terrorist potential, we need to adopt new policies and strategies that will prevent some of the criminal activities so as to prevent terrorism. As we have seen, involvement in petty crimes leads to major crimes in some cases. Targeting males between the ages of 15 and 25 with past history of crime who suddenly become religious fundamentalists is highly recommended. In the final analysis, theories of violent political culture, theories of crime causation, and research by other scholars support my claim that there is a possible link between past criminality and terrorist potential. As we have seen in this chapter, there are many pathways through which terrorist groups end. Al-Qaeda, as mentioned earlier will eventually disintegrate.

END NOTES

1 Timothy Lynch, "The Case Against Plea Bargaining." *Regulation,* no. 3, vol. 26 (Washington D.C.: Cato Institute, Fall 2003), 27.

2 Stephen J. Schulhofer, "Is Plea Bargaining Inevitable?" *Harvard Law Review,* no. 5, vol. 97 (Cambridge: Harvard University Press, 1984), 1037.

3 John H. Langbein, "Torture and Plea Bargaining." *University of Chicago Law Review,* no. 1, vol. 46 (University of Chicago, Autumn, 1978), 9.

4 Langbein, "Torture and Plea Bargaining," 22.

5 Langbein, J. H. "The Plea," PBS Frontline, http://www.pbs.org/wgbh/pages/frontline/shows/plea/interviews/langbein.html.

6 Santobello v. New York, 404 U.S. 257, 261 (1971).

7 *Santobello,* 404 U.S. 257 at 261.

8 *Santobello,* 404 U.S. 257 at 261.

9 Santobello v. New York, 35 App Div 2d 1084, 316 N.Y.S. 2d 194 (1970).

10 *Santobello,* 404 U.S. 257at 257.

11 *Santobello,* 404 U.S. 257at 257

12 *Santobello*, 404 U.S. 257at 257

13 *Santobello,* 404 U.S. 257at 257

14 *Santobello,* 404 U.S. 257at 257

15 Federal Rules of Criminal Procedure, 11 (C)

16 Federal Rules of Criminal Procedure, 11.(e)(1)

17 Sarah N. Welling, "Victim Participation in Plea Bargains." *Washington University Law Quarterly*, no. 2, vol. 65 (Washington: University of Washington, 1987), 315.

18 Schlesinger and Malloy, "Plea Bargaining and the Judiciary; An Argument for Reform." *Drake Law Review*, vol. 30 (Des Moines: Drake University Law School, 1980), 581.

19 Welling, "Victim Participation in Plea Bargains," 316.

20 United States v. Adams, 634 F.2d 830 (5th Cir. 1981).

21 *Adams,* 634 F.2d at 836.

22 *Adams*, 634 F.2d at 842.

23 Boykin v. Alabama, 395 U.S. 238, (1969).

24 McCarthy v. United States, 394 U.S. 459 (1969).

25 Boykin v. Alabama, 395 U.S. 238; 89 S. Ct. 1709; 23 L. Ed. 2d 274; U.S. LEXIS 1434 (1969).

26 *Boykin,* 395 U.S. 238 at 238.

END NOTES

[27] *Boykin,* 395 U.S. 238 at 242.
[28] *Boykin*, 395 U.S. 238 at 242.
[29] *Boykin,* 395 U.S. 238 at 242.
[30] *Boykin,* 395 U.S. 238 at 242.
[31] *McCarthy,* 394 U.S. 459 at 459.
[32] *McCarthy,* 394 U.S. 459 at 459.
[33] *McCarthy,* 394 U.S. 459 at 459.
[34] *McCarthy,* 394 U.S. 459 at 463.
[35] *McCarthy,* 394 U.S. 459 at 467.
[36] *McCarthy,* 394 U.S. 459 at 471.
[37] Brady v. United States, 397 U.S. 742 (1970).
[38] *Brady,* 397 U.S. 742 at 742.
[39] *Brady,* 397 U.S. 742 at 742.
[40] *Brady,* 397 U.S. 742 at 742.
[41] *Brady,* 397 U.S. 742 at 742.
[42] *Brady,* 397 U.S. 742 at 742.
[43] *Brady,* 397 U.S. 742 at 742.
[44] *Brady,* 397 U.S. 742 at 742.
[45] *Brady,* 397 U.S. 742 at 756.
[46] Henderson v. Morgan, 426 U.S. 637 (1976).
[47] *Henderson* , 426 U.S. 637 at 637.
[48] *Henderson,* 426 U.S. 637 at 641.
[49] *Henderson,* 426 U.S. 637 at 641.
[50] *Henderson,* 426 U.S. 637 at 638.
[51] *Henderson,* 426 U.S. 637 at 638.
[52] *Henderson,* 426 U.S. 637 at 638.
[53] *Henderson,* 426 U.S. 637 at 637.
[54] *Henderson,* 426 U.S. 637 at 647.
[55] *Henderson,* 426 U.S. 637 at 647.
[56] *Henderson,* 426 U.S. 637 at 647.
[57] Joshua Dressler, *Understanding Criminal Procedure.* 2nd ed. (New York: Mathew Bender 1997), 564.
[58] Godinez v. Moran, 509 U.S. 389 (1993).
[59] Dressler, *Understanding Criminal Procedure,* 561.
[60] James E. Bond, *Plea Bargaining and Guilty Pleas* (New York: Clark Boardman 1975), 11.
[61] Mary E. Vogel, "The Social Origins of Plea Bargaining: Conflict and the Law in the Process of State Formation, 1830 – 1860." *Law and Society Review,* no. 1, vol. 33 (New Jersey: John Wiley 1999), 161.
[62] Vogel, "The Social Origins of Plea Bargaining," 163.

END NOTES

[63] Vogel, "The Social Origins of Plea Bargaining," 235.
[64] Vogel, "The Social Origins of Plea Bargaining," 235.
[65] Lawrence M. Friedman, "Plea Bargaining in Historical Perspective." *Law and Society Review,* no. 2, vol. 13 (New Jersey: John Wiley, Winter 1979), 247.
[66] Friedman, "Plea Bargaining in Historical Perspective," 247.
[67] Friedman, "Plea Bargaining in Historical Perspective," 5.
[68] Albert W. Alschuler, "Plea Bargaining and Its History." *Law and Society Review,* no. 2, vol. 13 (New Jersey: John Wiley, Winter 1979), 221.
[69] Alschuler, "Plea Bargaining and Its History," 221.
[70] Alschuler, "Plea Bargaining and Its History," 221.
[71] Alschuler, "Plea Bargaining and Its History," 242.
[72] Alschuler, "Plea Bargaining and Its History," 224.
[73] Commonwealth v. Battis, 1 Mass. 95 (1804).
[74] *Battis,* 1 Mass. 95 (1804).
[75] Swang v. State, 42 Tenn. (2 Caldwell) 212 (1865).
[76] Wight v. Rindskpof, 43 Wis. 344, 354-55, (1877).
[77] Edward v. People, 39 Mich. 760 (1878).
[78] State v. Richardson, 12 S.W. 245 (Mo. 1889).
[79] Unites States v. Jackson, 390 U.S. 570 (1968.)
[80] United States v. Jackson, 390 .U.S. 570; 88 S. Ct. 1209; 20 L. Ed. 2d 138; U.S. LEXIS 2002(1968).
[81] *Jackson,* 390 U.S. 570 at 572.
[82] *Jackson,* 390 U.S. 570 at 581.
[83] *Jackson,* 390 U.S. 570 at 583.
[84] *Jackson,* 390 U.S. 570 at 591.
[85] *Brady, 397 U.S. 742 at 742.*
[86] North Carolina v. Alford, 400 U.S. 25; 91 S. Ct. 160, 164 (1970).
[87] *Alford,* 91 S. Ct. 160 at 164.
[88] *Alford,* 91 S. Ct. 160 at 171.
[89] *Alford,* 91 S. Ct. 160 at 172.
[90] *Alford,* 91 S. Ct. 160 at 160.
[91] *Santobello,* 404 U.S. 257 at 260.
[92] *Santobello,* 404 U.S. 257 at 260.
[93] *Santobello,* 404 U.S. 257 at 260.
[94] *Santobello,* 404 U.S. 257 at 260.
[95] Roland Acevedo, "Is a Ban on Plea Bargaining an Ethical Abuse of Discretion? A Bronx County, New York Case Study." *Fordham Law*

Review, no. 3, vol. 64 (New York: Fordham University School of Law, 1995), 990.

[96] Friedman, "Plea Bargaining in Historical Perspective," 251.

[97] Ralph A. Fine, "Plea Bargaining: An Unnecessary Evil." *Marquette Law Review,* no. 623, vol. 70 (Milwaukee: Marquette University School of Law, Summer 1987), 631.

[98] Fine, "Plea Bargaining: An Unnecessary Evil," 631.

[99] Fine, "Plea Bargaining: An Unnecessary Evil," 632.

[100] Fine, "Plea Bargaining: An Unnecessary Evil," 20/6.

[101] Kenneth Kipnis, "Criminal Justice and the Negotiated Plea." Ethics, no. 2, vol. 86 (Chicago: The University of Chicago, January 1976), 93.

[102] Stephen Schulhofer, "The Plea," PBS Frontline, http://pbs.org/wgbh/pages/frontline/shows/plea/interviews/schulhofer.html.

[103] Oren Gazal-Ayal, "Partial Ban on Plea Bargains." *Cardozo Law Review,* no. 5, vol. 27 (New York: Benjamin Cardozo School of Law, 2006), 2295.

[104] Gazal-Ayal, "Partial Ban on Plea Bargains," 2295.

[105] Gerald D. Robin, *Introduction to the Criminal Justice System.* 3rd ed. (New York: HarperCollins, 1987), 249.

[106] Alschuler, "Implementing the Criminal Defendant's Right to Trial," 934.

[107] Robin, *Introduction to the Criminal Justice System*, 253.

[108] Chad Baruch, "Through the Looking Glass: A Brief Comment on the Short Life and Unhappy Demise of the Singleton Rule." *Northern Kentucky Law Review,* no. 4, vol. 27 (Kentucky: Northern Kentucky University, 2000), 851.

[109] Joseph A. Colquitt, "Ad Hoc Plea Bargaining." *Tulane Law Review*, no. 1, vol. 75 (New Orleans: Tulane University Law School, 2001), 704.

[110] Robin, *Introduction to the Criminal Justice System,* 259.

[111] Robin, *Introduction to the Criminal Justice System,* 257.

[112] Robin, *Introduction to the Criminal Justice System,* 257.

[113] Frank H. Easterbrook, "Plea Bargaining as Compromise." *The Yale Law Journal,* no. 8, vol. 101 (New Haven, CT: The Yale Law Journal Company, June 1992), 1969.

[114] Baruch, "Through the Looking Glass," 849.

END NOTES

[115] Jennifer Mnookin, "Uncertain Bargains: The Rise of Plea Bargaining in America," *Stanford Law Review,* no. 3, vol. 57 (Stanford, CA: Stanford University, 2005), 1722.

[116] Kipnis, "Criminal Justice and the Negotiated Plea," 93.

[117] Langbein, "Torture and Plea Bargaining,"18.

[118] John Langbein, "The Plea."

[119] Langbein, "The Plea."

[120] Langbein, "The Plea."

[121] Langbein, "The Plea."

[122] Timothy Sandefur, "In Defense of Plea Bargaining," *Regulation,* no. 3, vol. 26 (Washington D.C: The Cato Institute, Fall 2003), 28.

[123] Sandefur, "In Defense of Plea Bargaining," 28.

[124] Albert W. Alschuler, "Straining at Gnats and Swallowing Camels: The Selective Morality of Professor Bibas," *Cornell Law Review,* no. 5, vol. 88 (New York: Cornell Law School, July 2003) 1413.

[125] Alschuler, "Straining at Gnats and Swallowing Camels," 1413.

[126] Alschuler, "Straining at Gnats and Swallowing Camels," 1413.

[127] Langbein, J. H., "The Plea."

[128] Robert E. Scott, and William J. Stuntz, "Plea Bargaining as Contract," *Yale Law Journal,* vol. 101 (New Haven, CT: The Yale Law Journal Company, 1992), 1912.

[129] Mark E. Cammack and Norman M. Garland, *Advanced Criminal Procedure* (St. Paul, Mn: Thomson West, 2006), 274.

[130] Cammack and Garland, *Advanced Criminal Procedure,* 272.

[131] Cammack and Norman M. Garland, *Advanced Criminal Procedure,* 272.

[132] Missouri v. Frye, 132 S.Ct. 1399 (2012).

[133] Lafler v. Cooper, U.S. 132 S.Ct. 1378, L.Ed.2d (2012).

[134] *Frye,* 132 S.Ct. 1399.

[135] *Frye,* 132 S.Ct. 1399.

[136] *Frye,* 132 S.Ct. 1399.

[137] Baruch, *Through the Looking Glass,* 849.

[138] Stephen J. Schulhofer, "Plea Bargaining as Disaster," *Yale Law Journal,* vol. 101 (New Haven, CT: The Yale Law Journal Company, June 1992), 1979.

[139] Schulhofer, "Plea Bargaining as Disaster," 1979.

[140] Alschuler, "Implementing the Criminal Defendant's Right to Trial," 933.

[141] Cammack and Garland, *Advanced Criminal Procedure,* 272.

[142] Cammack and Garland, *Advanced Criminal Procedure,* 272.

END NOTES

[143] Sam W. Callan, "An Experience in Justice without Plea Negotiation," *Law and Society Review,* vol. 13 (New Jersey: John Wiley, 1979), 327.

[144] Bordenkircher v. Hayes, 434 U.S. 357, 359; 98 S. Ct. 663; 54 L. Ed. 2d 604; U.S. LEXIS 56(1978).

[145] *Bordenkircher,* 434 U.S. 357 at 359.

[146] *Bordenkircher,* 434 U.S. 357 at 359.

[147] *Bordenkircher,* 434 U.S. 357 at 359.

[148] *Bordenkircher,* 434 U.S. 357 at 359.

[149] *Bordenkircher,* 434 U.S. 357 at 366.

[150] *Bordenkircher,* 434 U.S. 357 at 367.

[151] *Bordenkircher,* 434 U.S. 357 at 368.

[152] *Bordenkircher,* 434 U.S. 357 at 373.

[153] Fine, "Plea Bargaining: An Unnecessary Evil," 615.

[154] Fine, "Plea Bargaining: An Unnecessary Evil," 616.

[155] Fine, "Plea Bargaining: An Unnecessary Evil," 616.

[156] Fine, "Plea Bargaining: An Unnecessary Evil," 617.

[157] Fine, "Plea Bargaining: An Unnecessary Evil," 618.

[158] State v. Brown, 758 N.W. 2d 594; Minn. App. LEXIS 388(2008).

[159] *Brown*, 758 N.W. 2d at 595.

[160] Federal Rules of Evidence 410: Inadmissibility of Pleas, Plea Discussions, and Related Statements.

[161] *State v. Brown, 758 N.W. 2d 594; 2008 Minn. App. LEXIS 388*

[162] *Brown,* 758 N.W. 2d at 598.

[163] *Brown,* 758 N.W. 2d at 599.

[164] *Brown,* 758 N.W. 2d at 594.

[165] *Brown,* 758 N.W. 2d at 594.

[166] *Brown*, 758 N.W. 2d at 598.

[167] *Brown*, 758 N.W. 2d at 596.

[168] State v. Brown, No. A07-599, Supreme Court of Minnesota, (January 05, 2011).

[169] "Killer to Receive Calzones, Pizza With Life Sentence, FOXNEWS.COM,http://www.foxnews.com/story/0,2933,399207,00.html

[170] Clemente Lisi, "Feeding a Killer Appetite," *New York Post,* http://www.nypost.com/seven/08082008/news/regionalnews/feeding_a_killer_appetite_123567.htm,

[171] Aimee Green, "Prisoner Trades Chicken Dinner for Guilty Plea in Killing," Oregonlive.com, http://www.oregonlive.com/news/oregonian/index.ssf?/base/news/12

17044564193670.xml&coll=7

[172] see, id.

[173] David Kravets, "Judge Says Reiser Rejected 3-Year Plea Offer, Remains Skeptical of Deal Unearthing Nina," Wired.com, http://www.wired.com/threatlevel/2008/07/judge-says-reis/

[174] ABA Standards for Criminal Justice, Pleas of Guilty, 3rd Ed., (Chicago: American Bar Association, 1999),14-3.1(e).

[175] Welling, Victim Participation in Plea Bargains, 304.

[176] Welling, Victim Participation in Plea Bargains, 304.

[177] Welling, "Victim Participation in Plea Bargains," 310.

[178] Welling, "Victim Participation in Plea Bargains," 310.

[179] Welling, "Victim Participation in Plea Bargains," 355.

[180] Welling, "Victim Participation in Plea Bargains," 355.

[181] Welling, "Victim Participation in Plea Bargains," 355.

[182] Welling, "Victim Participation in Plea Bargains," 355.

[183] Stephen J. Schulhofer, "The Plea."

[184] Alschuler, "Implementing the Criminal Defendant's Right to Trial," 936.

[185] Whitney S. Hibbard, Raymond. W. Worring, and Richard S. Brennan, *Psychic Criminology: A Guide for Using Psychics in Investigations*, (Springfield: Charles C. Thomas Publishers, 2002), 22.

[186] What is Parapsychology? (Columbus, OH: Parapsychological Association), http://www.parapsych.org/faq_file1.html

[187] Susan Blackmore, "Parapsychology," in Colman., A. M., (Eds.), *Controversies in Psychology*, (New York: Longman, 1995), 2nd Ed, 1.

[188] Hibbard et al, *Psychic Criminology: A Guide for Using Psychics in Investigations,* 24.

[189] Hibbard et al, Psychic Criminology: A Guide for Using Psychics in Investigations, 24.

[190] Hibbard et al, *Psychic Criminology: A Guide for Using Psychics in Investigations,* 25.

[191] Hibbard et al, Psychic Criminology: A Guide for Using Psychics in Investigations, 25.

[192] Roll, W. G., and Williams, B. J., "Quantum Theory, Neurobiology, and Parapsychology," in Stanley Krippner and Harris L. Friedman, *Mysterious Minds: The Neurobiology of Psychics, Mediums, and Other Extraordinary People*, (Santa Barbara, CA: Praeger, 2010), 23.

END NOTES

[193] Roll and Williams, "Quantum Theory, Neurobiology, and Parapsychology," 23.
[194] Roll and Williams, "Quantum Theory, Neurobiology, and Parapsychology," 23.
[195] Roll and Williams, "Quantum Theory, Neurobiology, and Parapsychology," 23.
[196] Roll and Williams, "Quantum Theory, Neurobiology, and Parapsychology," 23.
[197] Roll and Williams, "Quantum Theory, Neurobiology, and Parapsychology," 23.
[198] Russell Targ and Jane E. Katra, "Remote Viewing in a Group Setting." *Journal of Scientific Exploration,* no. 1, vol. 10 (Petaluma, CA: Society for Scientific Exploration, 2000), 108.
[199] Targ and Katra, "Remote Viewing in a Group Setting," 108.
[200] Targ and Katra, "Remote Viewing in a Group Setting," 109.
[201] Russell Targ, "Remote Viewing at Stanford Research Institute in the 1970's: A Memoir." *Journal of Scientific Exploration,* no. 1, vol. 10 (Petaluma, CA: Society for Scientific Exploration, 1996), 77.
[202] Targ, "Remote Viewing at Stanford Research Institute in the 1970's: A Memoir," 77.
[203] Targ, "Remote Viewing at Stanford Research Institute in the 1970's: A Memoir," 78.
[204] Targ, "Remote Viewing at Stanford Research Institute in the 1970's: A Memoir," 78.
[205] Arthur Lyons and Marcello Truzzi, *The Blue Sense: Psychic Detectives and Crime,* (New York: The Mysterious Press, 1991), 9.
[206] Hibbard et al, *Psychic Criminology: A Guide for Using Psychics in Investigations,* 24.
[207] Hibbard et al, *Psychic Criminology: A Guide for Using Psychics in Investigations*, 24.
[208] Hibbard et al, *Psychic Criminology: A Guide for Using Psychics in Investigations,* 25.
[209] The following discussion draws from the work of Lyons and Truzzi, *The Blue Sense: Psychic Detectives and Crime.*
[210] Hibbard et al, Psychic Criminology: A Guide for Using Psychics in Investigations, 18.
[211] Fillipus Brink, "Parapsychology and Criminal Investigation." *International Criminal Police Review*, (Lyon, France: Saint Cloud, ICPO, January 1960) 3.
[212] see, Brink, "Parapsychology and Criminal Investigation," 4.

END NOTES

[213] Lyons and Truzzi, *The Blue Sense: Psychic Detectives and Crime,* 32.

[214] Lyons and Truzzi, *The Blue Sense: Psychic Detectives and Crime,* 29.

[215] Lyons and Truzzi, *The Blue Sense: Psychic Detectives and Crime,* 29.

[216] Lyons and Truzzi, *The Blue Sense: Psychic Detectives and Crime,* 29.

[217] Hibbard et al, *Psychic Criminology: A Guide for Using Psychics in Investigations,* 12.

[218] Hibbard et al, *Psychic Criminology: A Guide for Using Psychics in Investigations,* 14.

[219] Robin Woffitt, *The Language of Mediums and Psychics: The Social Organization of Everyday Miracles,*(Aldershot: Ashgate, 2006), 7.

[220] Lyons and Truzzi, *The Blue Sense: Psychic Detectives and Crime,* 64.

[221] Luis A. Cordon, *Popular Psychology: An Encyclopedia,* (Westport, CT: Greenwood Press, 2005),182.

[222] Combs, A., 'Forward, ' *in* Stanley Krippner and Harris L. Friedman, *Mysterious Minds: The Neurobiology of Psychics, Mediums, and Other Extraordinary People, (Santa Barbara, CA: Praeger, 2010), x.*

[223] Roll and Williams, "Quantum Theory, Neurobiology, and Parapsychology, " 1.

[224] Roll and Williams, "Quantum Theory, Neurobiology, and Parapsychology," 2.

[225] Roll and Williams, "Quantum Theory, Neurobiology, and Parapsychology," 3.

[226] Roll and Williams, "Quantum Theory, Neurobiology, and Parapsychology," 3.

[227] Roll and Williams, "Quantum Theory, Neurobiology, and Parapsychology," 3.

[228] Roll and Williams, "Quantum Theory, Neurobiology, and Parapsychology," 3.

[229] Roll and Williams, "Quantum Theory, Neurobiology, and Parapsychology," 3.

[230] Roll and Williams, "Quantum Theory, Neurobiology, and Parapsychology," 3.

[231] see, Roll and Williams, "Quantum Theory, Neurobiology, and Parapsychology," 3.

END NOTES

232 Roll and Williams, "Quantum Theory, Neurobiology, and Parapsychology," 3.
233 Roll and Williams, "Quantum Theory, Neurobiology, and Parapsychology," 8.
234 Roll and Williams, "Quantum Theory, Neurobiology, and Parapsychology," 8.
235 Roll and Williams, "Quantum Theory, Neurobiology, and Parapsychology," 8.
236 Roll and Williams, "Quantum Theory, Neurobiology, and Parapsychology," 23.
237 Roll and Williams, "Quantum Theory, Neurobiology, and Parapsychology," 23.
238 Joan H. Hageman., Julio F. P. Peres., Alexander Moreira-Almeida, Leonardo Caixeta, Ian Wickramasekera 11 , and Stanley Krippner. "The Neurobiology of Trance and Mediumship in Brazil," in Krippner S., and Friedman, H. L., "Mysterious Minds: The Neurobiology of Psychics, Mediums, and Other Extraordinary People, 89 (2010), citing the work of Azari et al., 2001; Beauregard and Paquette, 2006; Jevning et al ., 1996; Newberg et al., 2001; Newberg et al., 2003; Newberg et al, 2006. Not sure what this note is for but a lot of this info is very confusing, and it is not presented in the correct form. I honestly don't even know how to fix this. Please refer to the Chicago manual for proper citations.
239 See, Hageman et al, "The Neurobiology of Trance and Mediumship in Brazil,"89.
240 See, Hageman et al, "The Neurobiology of Trance and Mediumship in Brazil," 89.
241 Hageman et al, "The Neurobiology of Trance and Mediumship in Brazil," 89.
242 [Reprinted from the Journal of Scientific Exploration, 10(1), 89-90, "The American Institutes for Research Review of the Department of Defense's STAR GATE Program: A Commentary," by Edwin C. May, published by the Society for Scientific Exploration, www.scientificexploration.org]. Copyright Edwin C. May (1996), reprinted with permission. Not sure what to make of this note either or the ones following.
243 id.
244 [Reprinted from the Journal of Scientific Exploration, 10(1), 90-91, "The American Institutes for Research Review of the Department of

Defense's STAR GATE Program: A Commentary," by Edwin C. May, published by the Society for Scientific Exploration, www.scientificexploration.org]. Copyright Edwin C. May (1996), reprinted with permission.

245 [Reprinted from the Journal of Scientific Exploration, 10(1), 106, "The American Institutes for Research Review of the Department of Defense's STAR GATE Program: A Commentary," by Edwin C. May, published by the Society for Scientific Exploration, www.scientificexploration.org]. Copyright Edwin C. May (1996), reprinted with permission.

246 see, Hibbard et al, *Psychic Criminology: A Guide for Using Psychics in Investigations,* 10-21.

247 Hibbard et al, *Psychic Criminology: A Guide for Using Psychics in Investigations,* 10-21.

248 Lyons and Truzzi, *The Blue Sense: Psychic Detectives and Crime,* back cover.

249 Lyons and Truzzi, *The Blue Sense: Psychic Detectives and Crime,* 2.

250 Lyons and Truzzi, *The Blue Sense: Psychic Detectives and Crime,* 2.

251 Lyons and Truzzi, *The Blue Sense: Psychic Detectives and Crime,* 2.

252 Lyons and Truzzi, *The Blue Sense: Psychic Detectives and Crime,* 89.

253 Lyons and Truzzi, *The Blue Sense: Psychic Detectives and Crime,* 284.

254 Lyons and Truzzi, *The Blue Sense: Psychic Detectives and Crime,* 285.

255 Lyons and Truzzi, *The Blue Sense: Psychic Detectives and Crime,* 285.

256 Lyons and Truzzi, *The Blue Sense: Psychic Detectives and Crime,* 286.

257 Hibbard et al, *Psychic Criminology: A Guide for Using Psychics in Investigations,* 132.

258 Hibbard et al, *Psychic Criminology: A Guide for Using Psychics in Investigations,* 131.

259 Hibbard et al, *Psychic Criminology: A Guide for Using Psychics in Investigations,* 21.

260 Hugo Meynell, "On Investigation of the So-called Paranormal," in Stoeber, M., and Meynell, H., (Eds.) *Critical Reflections on the Paranormal,* (Albany, NY: State University of New York Press, 1996), 40.

END NOTES

[261] Michael D. Risinger and Jeffrey L. Loop, "Three Card Monte, Monty Hall, Modus Operandi and "Offender Profiling": Some Lessons of Modern Cognitive Science for the Law of Evidence," *Cardozo Law Review,* no. 2, vol. 24 (New York Benjamin Cardozo School of Law, 2002), 193-285.

[262] Laurence Alison, Matthew Smith and Keith Morgan, "Interpreting the Accuracy of Offender Profiles." *Psychology, Crime and Law,* no. 2, vol. 9 (New York: Routledge, 2003), 185-195.

[263] Alison et al, "Interpreting the Accuracy of Offender Profiles," 194.

[264] Danny J. MacDonald and Lionel G. Standing, "Does Self-Serving Bias Cancel the Barnum Effect?" Social *Behavior and Personality: An International Journal,* no. 1, vol. 30 (Palmerston North, New Zealand, 2002), 626.

[265] MacDonald and Standing, "Does Self-Serving Bias Cancel the Barnum Effect?," 625.

[266] Andre A. Moenssens, "Novel Scientific Evidence in Criminal Cases: Some Words of Caution," *Journal of Criminal Law and Criminology,* no. 1, vol. 84 (Chicago: Northwestern University School of Law, Spring 1993), 4.

[267] Frye v. United States, 293 F, 1013, 1014, (D.C. Cir. 1923).

[268] *Frye,* 293 F, 1013 at 1013.

[269] Federal Rules of Evidence, 702.

[270] Federal Rules of Evidence, 702.

[271] Federal Rules of Evidence, 702.

[272] Jason Dearen, "Testimony will be Limited to Witness Career to Establish Credibility, not Validity of Mediums," InsideBayArea.com, http://www.insidebayarea.com/oaklandtribune/ci_3908618

[273] Jesse McKinley, "Conviction Concludes Bizzarre Trial for Murder," *New York Times*, June 17, 2006.

[274] Carol Pogash, "A California Murder Case Raises Troubling Issues," *New York Times,* September 18, 2005.

[275] Juan Ignacio Blanco, 'Murderpedia: The Encyclopedia of Murderers," http://murderpedia.org/female.P/p/polk-susan.htm

[276] Dearen, "Testimony will be Limited to Witness Career to Establish Credibility, not Validity of Mediums."

[277] Bob Egelko, "Susan Polk's Conviction Upheld," *San Francisco Gate,* (San Francisco: San Francisco Chronicle, December 14, 2010), http://articles.sfgate.com/2010-12-14/bay-area/25190181_1_murder-conviction-appeals-court-juror-misconduct.

END NOTES

[278] Egelko, "Susan Polk's Conviction Upheld."

[279] Polk v. The First District Court of Appeal, U.S. Dist. LEXIS 130346(2009).

[280] *Polk*, U.S. Dist. LEXIS 130346

[281] *Polk,* U.S. Dist. LEXIS 130346

[282] Shannon Frattaroli, Daniel W. Webster and Stephen P. Teret. "Unintentional Gun Injuries, Firearm Design, and Prevention: What We Know, What We Need to Know, and What Can Be Done," *Journal of Urban Health:* Bulletin of the New York Academy of Medicine, no. 1, vol. 79 (New York: New York Academy of Medicine, March 2002), 54.

[283] Garen Wintemute, "The Relationship Between Firearm Design and Firearm Violence." *Journal of the American Medical Association*, no. 22, vol. 275 (Chicago: American Medical Association, June 1996), 1749.

[284] Frederick P. Rivara, and Arthur, L. Kellerman, "Reducing the Misuse of Firearms," In Lynda S. Doll, Sandra E. Bonzo, James A. Mercy, and David A. Sleet (Eds.), Handbook of Injury and Violence Prevention, (New York: Springer, 2007), 319.

[285] Frattaroli et al, "Unintentional Gun Injuries, Firearm Design, and Prevention," 50.

[286] see, Frattaroli et al, "Unintentional Gun Injuries, Firearm Design, and Prevention," 50.

[287] Frattaroli et al, "Unintentional Gun Injuries, Firearm Design, and Prevention," 51.

[288] Frattaroli et al, "Unintentional Gun Injuries, Firearm Design, and Prevention," 51.

[289] see, Frattaroli et al, "Unintentional Gun Injuries, Firearm Design, and Prevention," 52.

[290] see, Frattaroli et al, "Unintentional Gun Injuries, Firearm Design, and Prevention," 51.

[291] Nancy Sinauer, Joseph Annest and James Mercy, "Unintentional, Nonfatal Firearm-Related Injuries." *Journal of the American Medical Association,* no. 22, vol. 275 (Chicago: American Medical Association , June 12, 1996), 1740.

[292] Cynthia Leonardatos, Paul H. Blackman, and David B. Kopel, "Smart Guns/Foolish Legislators: Finding the Right Public Safety Laws, and Avoiding the Wrong Ones." *Connecticut Law Review,* no. 1, vol. 34 (Hartford, CT: University of Connecticut School of Law, Fall 2001), 187.

END NOTES

293 Leonardatos et al, "Smart Guns/Foolish Legislators," 187.
294 Leonardatos et al, "Smart Guns/Foolish Legislators," 182.
295 Leonardatos et al, "Smart Guns/Foolish Legislators," 182.
296 Weiss, D. R., *Sandia National Laboratories, Smart Gun Technology Project: Final Report,* (Albuquerque, NM: Sandia National Laboratories, 1996), 7.
297 Leonardatos et al, "Smart Guns/Foolish Legislators," 183.
298 Leonardatos et al, "Smart Guns/Foolish Legislators" 183.
299 www.tarnhelm.com (Accessed 07/24/13).
300 Magna-Trigger Gun Safety, www.tarnhelm.com
301 id.
302 Leonardatos et al, "Smart Guns/Foolish Legislators," 184.
303 Leonardatos et al, "Smart Guns/Foolish Legislators," 184.
304 Leonardatos et al, "Smart Guns/Foolish Legislators," 184.
305 Leonardatos et al, "Smart Guns/Foolish Legislators," 185.
306 Leonardatos et al, "Smart Guns/Foolish Legislators," 185.
307 Leonardatos et al, "Smart Guns/Foolish Legislators," 192.
308 Leonardatos et al, "Smart Guns/Foolish Legislators," 192.
309 Leonardatos et al, "Smart Guns/Foolish Legislators," 192.
310 Leonardatos et al, "Smart Guns/Foolish Legislators," 195.
311 Leonardatos et al, "Smart Guns/Foolish Legislators," 195.
312 Stephen P. Teret, Daniel W. Webster, Jon S. Vernick, Tom W. Smith, Garen J. Wintemute, Philip J. Cook, Darnell F. Hawkins, Arthur L. Kellerman, Susan B. Sorenson, and Susan DeFrancesco. "Support for New Policies to Regulate Firearms." *New England Journal of Medicine*, no. 12, vol. 339 (Boston: NEJM Group, September 17, 1998), 813-818.
313 Teret et al, "Support for New Policies to Regulate Firearms," 813.
314 Teret et al,"Support for New Policies to Regulate Firearms," 815.
315 Teret et al, "Support for New Policies to Regulate Firearms," 815.
316 Susan B. Sorenson, "Regulating Firearms as a Consumer Product." *Science,* no. 5444, vol. 286 (Washington D.C: American Association for the Advancement of Science, November 19, 1999), 1482.
317 Such states include Massachusetts and New Jersey.
318 Leonardatos et al, "Smart Guns/Foolish Legislators," 199.
319 Leonardatos et al, "Smart Guns/Foolish Legislators," 199.
320 Frattaroli et al, "Unintentional Gun Injuries, Firearm Design, and Prevention," 56.
321 Leonardatos et al, "Smart Guns/Foolish Legislators," 219.
322 Teret et al, "Support for New Policies to Regulate Firearms," 815.

END NOTES

[323] Leslie Wayne, "Smart" Guns Prove to be No Quick Fix for Firearm Violence. " New York Times, (New York: New York Times, June 15, 1999). A24.

[324] Steve Friess, "NRA: Smart Guns Are Plain Stupid," Wired.com, www.wired.com/print/politics/law/news/2002/04/52178

[325] see, id.

[326] Ultrascan Advanced Global Investigations, "419 Victims & Global Losses," http://www.ultrascan-agi.com/public_html/html/419_Victims_and_Global_Losses.html

[327] Blaise J. Bergiel, Erick B. Bergiel, and Philip W. Balsmeier, "Internet Cross Border Crime: A Growing Problem." *Journal of Website Promotion*, no. 3, vol. 3 (Oxford: Haworth Press, 2008), 135.

[328] United States Code: Title 18, Part 1, Chapter 95, s 1953. Interstate transportation of wagering paraphernalia.

[329] Federal Trade Commission, "International Lottery Scams." (Washington D.C: Federal Trade Commission, January 2006.), FTC Consumer Alert.

[330] Bergiel et al, "Internet Cross Border Crime: A Growing Problem," 136.

[331] Andrew Stevens, *"419" The Story of the Advance Fee Fraud.* (Frederick, MD: Publish America, 2006), 13.

[332] Stevens, *"419" The Story of the Advance Fee Fraud,* 11.

[333] Stevens, *"419" The Story of the Advance Fee Fraud*, 76.

[334] Esharenana E. Adomi, and Stella E. Igun, "Combating Cyber Crime in Nigeria." *The Electronic Library,* no. 5, vol. 26 (Bingley, United Kingdom, Emerald Insights Group Publishing, 2008), 719.

[335] Mitchell Zuckoff, "The Perfect Mark: How a Massachusetts Psychotherapist Fell for a Nigerian E-mail Scam." *The New Yorker,* (New York: Conde Nast, May 15, 2006).

[336] U.S. Department of State website.

[337] The Federal Bureau of Investigations, "Common Fraud Schemes," (Washington D.C: www.fbi.gov/majcases/fraud/fraudschemes.htm

[338] Charles Tive, *419 Scam Exploits of the Nigerian Con Man.* (Bloomington, IN: iuniverse, inc., 2006), 83.

[339] Tive, *419 Scam Exploits of the Nigerian Con Man*, 84.

[340] Federal Trade Commission, "FTC Releases Consumer Fraud Survey," (Washington D.C: Federal Trade Commission, Press Release, October 29, 2007).

[341] id.

END NOTES

342 id.

343 Brian Ross, and Joseph Rhee, "Former Congressman Duped by Nigerian Scams." ABC News, December 8, 2006. http://blogs.abcnews.com/theblotter/2006/12/father_of_chels.html

344 id.

345 Anna Song, "Woman Out $400K to 'Nigerian Scam' Con Artists." KATU News, November 21, 2008, http://www.katu.com/news/34292654.html

346 id.

347 id.

348 id.

349 id.

350 Attorney General, State of Michigan, "Former Alcona County Treasurer Sentenced to 9-14 Years in Nigerian Scam Case," Press Release, June 12, 2007.

351 Attorney General, State of Michigan, "Former Alcona County Treasurer Charged with Embezzling Public Monies," Press Release, January 17, 2007.

352 id.

353 Attorney General, State of Michigan, "Former Alcona County Treasurer Sentenced to 9-14 Years in Nigerian Scam Case," Press Release, June 12, 2007.

354 id.

355 id.

356 see, Bergiel et al, "Internet Cross Border Crime: A Growing Problem,"137.

357 id.

358 Jack Malvern, "Clever People Are Easier to Con," *The Times* (London: March 17, 2008).

359 Ultrascan Advanced Global Investigations, "419 Advance Fee Fraud Statistics 2009," http://www.ultrascan-agi.com/public_html/html/419_fraud_trends_2006.html

360 id.

361 id.

362 id.

363 id.

364 id.

365 id.

366 id.

367 id.

END NOTES

[368] Grossman, W., Untitled, *Computer Weekly,* 12, 5/4/2010.
[369] Metropolitan Police London, www.met.police.uk/fraudalert/419how_fraud.htm
[370] Taiwo A. Oriola, "Advance Fee Fraud on the Internet: Nigeria's Regulatory Response." *Computer Law and Security Review,* vol. 21 (Oxford: Elsevier, 2005), 245.
[371] Oriola, "Advance Fee Fraud on the Internet: Nigeria's Regulatory Response," 246.
[372] The Federal Bureau of Investigation, "Common Fraud Schemes," www.fbi.gov/majcases/fraud/fraudschemes.htm
[373] Department of Justice, "Nigerian National Found Guilty for Role in "Advance-Fee' Fraud Scheme," Press Release, Wednesday, March 24, 2010, http://www.justice.gov/opa/pr/2010/March/10-crm-306.html.
[374] id.
[375] Department of Justice, "Nigerian National Sentenced in North Carolina to 108 Months in Prison for Role in Advance Fee Fraud Scheme," Press Release, Thursday, February 24, 2011.
[376] id.
[377] id.
[378] Bank Scam Trial Opens in Nigeria, BBC News, http://news.bbc.co.uk/2/hi/africa/3460861.stm
[379] ThisDay, (Nigerian Newspaper) November 16, 2005.
[380] The Guardian, (Nigerian Newspaper) Saturday November 19, 2005.
[381] id.
[382] id.
[383] Jack Goldsmith, and TimWu, *Who Controls the Internet? Illusions of a Borderless World,* (Oxford: Oxford University Press, 2006), 70.
[384] Goldsmith and Wu, *Who Controls the Internet? Illusions of a Borderless World,* 73.
[385] Goldsmith and Wu, *Who Controls the Internet? Illusions of a Borderless World*, 73.
[386] Goldsmith and Wu, *Who Controls the Internet? Illusions of a Borderless World,* 74.
[387] Lawrence Lessig, *Code and Other Laws of Cyber Space* (New York: Basic Books, 1999), 43.
[388] Lessig, *Code and Other Laws of Cyber Space,* 49.
[389] Lessig, *Code and Other Laws of Cyber Space*, 50.
[390] Lessig, *Code and Other Laws of Cyber Space,* 50.
[391] Lessig, *Code and Other Laws of Cyber Space,*50-51.

END NOTES

[392] Ultrascan Advanced Global Investigations "419 Advance Fee Fraud Statistics 2009,", http://www.ultrascan-agi.com/public_html/html/__law_enforcement.html

[393] id.

[394] Louise Richardson, "The Roots of Terrorism: An Overview," in Louise Richardson, (eds.), *The Roots of Terrorism* (New York: Routledge, 2006), 2.

[395] The federal Bureau of Investigation, "FBI Policy and Guidelines," http://www.fbi.gov/publications/terror/terrorism2002_2005.pdf

[396] id.

[397] id.

[398] id, at 23.

[399] Andrew Silke, "Becoming a Terrorist," in Andrew Silke, (eds,), *Terrorists, Victims and Society: Psychological Perspectives on Terrorism and its Consequences* (Oxford: John Wiley, 2003), 33.

[400] Silke, "Becoming a Terrorist," 33.

[401] Rex A. Hudson, *The Sociology and Psychology of Terrorism: Who Becomes a Terrorist and Why?* (Washington, D.C: Library of Congress, 1999), 37.

[402] Audrey K. Cronin, "Sources of Contemporary Terrorism," in Audrey K. Cronin and James M. Ludes, (eds.), *Attacking Terrorism: Elements of a Grand Strategy* (Georgetown, Washington, D.C: Georgetown University Press, 2004), 24.

[403] Jerrold M. Post, "The Psychological Dynamics of Terrorism," in Louise Richardson (eds.), *The Roots of Terrorism,* (New York: Routledge, 2006), 18.

[404] Post, "The Psychological Dynamics of Terrorism," 18.

[405] Post, "The Psychological Dynamics of Terrorism," 26.

[406] Post, "The Psychological Dynamics of Terrorism," 26.

[407] John Horgan, "The Search for the Terrorist Personality," in Andrew Silke, (eds.), *Terrorists, Victims and Society: Psychological Perspectives on Terrorism and its Consequences* (Oxford: John Wiley, 2003), 5.

[408] Walter Laqueur, "Left, Right and Beyond: The Changing Face of Terror," In James Hoge, Jr., and Gideon Rose., (eds.), *How Did This Happen? Terrorism and the New War,* (New York: Public Affairs, 2001), 80.

[409] Horgan, "The Search for the Terrorist Personality," 23.

[410] Horgan, "The Search for the Terrorist Personality," 35.

[411] Horgan, "The Search for the Terrorist Personality," 35.

END NOTES

412 Horgan, "The Search for the Terrorist Personality," 35.
413 Horgan, "The Search for the Terrorist Personality," 37.
414 Saudi Interior Ministry Announces Names of Suspected Terrorists, June 28, 2005, http://www.saudinf.com/main/y8334.htm
415 Silke, "Becoming a Terrorist," 40.
416 Silke, "Becoming a Terrorist", 40.
417 James Gilligan, *Violence: Reflections on Our Deadliest Epidemic*, (London: Jessica Kingsley Publishers, 2000), 110.
418 Silke, "Becoming a Terrorist," 41.
419 Silke, "Becoming a Terrorist," 43.
420 Paul Hamilos, "Mass Murderers Jailed for 40 years as Judge Delivers Verdicts on Spain's 9/11." The Guardian, Wednesday October 31, 2007, http://www.guardian.co.uk/world/2007/nov/01/spain.international/print
421 Hamilos, "Mass Murderers Jailed for 40 years."
422 Zachary Coile, "Ordinary British Lads: Terror in London," (San Francisco: San Francisco Chronicle, July 14, 2005, http://www.sfgate.com/cgi-bin/article.cgi?f=/c/a/2005/07/14/MNGR7DNPP41& type.
423 Johnson, P., http://www.csmonitor.com/200/2006/0626/p01s01-ussc.htm?print=true
424 id.
425 id.
426 Michael Reynolds, "Chechnya: A Criminal Offense," *Asian Times,* November 28, 2002. http://www.atimes.com/atimes/Central_Asia/DK29Ag03.html
427 Reynolds, "Chechnya: A Criminal Offense."
428 Hudson, *The Sociology and Psychology of Terrorism,* 100.
429 Hudson, *The Sociology and Psychology of Terrorism,* 102.
430 Hudson, *The Sociology and Psychology of Terrorism,* 102.
431 Yvon Dandurand and Vivienne Chin, "Links between Terrorism and other Forms of Crime," A report submitted to Foreign Affairs Canada and The United Nations Office on Drugs and Crime, (British Columbia, Canada: International Centre For Criminal Law Reform, April 2004), 24.
432 Robert H. Jantzen "Dynamics of New York City Crime." Paper presented at the 66th International Atlantic Economic Conference, Montreal, Canada, October 2008.

END NOTES

[433] Randall Collins, "Suicide Bombers: Warriors of the Middle Class," *Foreign Policy* (Washington D.C: Foreign Policy Group, January 8, 2008).

[434] Cesare Lombroso, *The Criminal Man* (Turin: Fratella Boca, 1876).

[435] see, Alan Travis, "The Making of an Extremist," *Guardian,* Wednesday, August 20, 2008, http://www.guardian.co.uk/uk/2008/aug/20/uksecurity.terrorism/print

[436] Travis, "The Making of an Extremist."

[437] Jon Drummond, "Who Will Be Violent?; Correlates of Overt Activism and Criminality Among U.S. White Separatists," March 13, 2004. http://www.rcgd.isr.umich.edu/roots/Drummond %20Presentation.pdf

[438] Ustaz Mohammed Bin Ali, "Terrorism – The Outcome of a Culture of Hatred." http://www.pvtr.org/pdf/Ideology %20Response/Terrorism%20-%20The%20Outcome%20of%20a %20Culture%20of%20Hatred.pdf

[439] Rand Corporation, Press Release, *Rand Study Describes How West Can Counter Radical Islam.* (Santa Monica: Rand Corporation, March 18, 2004).

[440] Ustaz Mohammed Bin Ali, "Coping with the Threat of Jemaah Islamiyah – The Singapore Experience in Fighting Terrorism," (Singapore: International Centre for Political Violence and Terrorism Research, 2007).

[441] Leanard Weinberg and Arie Perliger, "How Terrorist Groups End," CTC Sentinel, no. 2, vol. 3 (West Point, New York: Combating Terrorism Center, February, 2010), 16.

[442] See Weinberg, L., and Perliger, A., "How Terrorist Groups End,' CTC Sentinel, no. 2, vol. 3, p.16, (February 2010). See also, Audrey K. Cronin, Ending Terrorism: Lessons for Policymakers from the Decline and Demise of Terrorist Groups, New York, Taylor and Francis, 2009.

[443] Audrey K. Cronin, "No Silver Bullets: Explaining Research on How Terrorism Ends," CTC Sentinel, no. 4, vol. 3 (West Point, New York: Combating Terrorism Center, April 2010), 16.

[444] Cronin, "No Silver Bullets: Explaining Research on How Terrorism Ends," 16.

[445] Cronin, "No Silver Bullets: Explaining Research on How Terrorism Ends," 16.

END NOTES

[446] Jones, S. G., and Martin C. Libicki, *How Terrorist Groups End: Lessons for Countering al Qai'da,* (Santa Monica: The Rand Corporation, 2008), xiv.

[447] Jones and Libicki, *How Terrorist Groups End: Lessons for Countering al Qai'da,* xiii.

[448] Jones and Libicki, *How Terrorist Groups End: Lessons for Countering al Qai'da,* xiii.

[449] Jones and Libicki, *How Terrorist Groups End: Lessons for Countering al Qai'da*, xiv.

[450] Jones and Libicki, *How Terrorist Groups End: Lessons for Countering al Qai'da*, xiv.

[451] Jones and Libicki, *How Terrorist Groups End: Lessons for Countering al Qai'da,* xiv.

[452] Jones and Libicki, *How Terrorist Groups End: Lessons for Countering al Qai'da,* xvii.

[453] Jones and Libicki, *How Terrorist Groups End: Lessons for Countering al Qai'da,* xiv – xv.

[454] National Strategy for Combating Terrorism, (Washington D.C: U.S Department of State 2006), 7.

[455] National Strategy for Combating Terrorism, 1.

[456] National Strategy for Combating Terrorism, 9.

[457] National Strategy for Combating Terrorism.

[458] Lora S. Aggour, "The Strategy of Containment in Fighting Terrorism," *Strategic Insights,* no. 4, vol. v11 (Monterey, CA: Center for Contemporary Conflict, Naval Postgraduate School, September 2008), 1.

[459] Hassan, "Key Considerations in Counterideological Work Against Terrorist Ideology," 531.

[460] Hassan, "Key Considerations in Counterideological Work Against Terrorist Ideology," 531.

[461] Hassan, "Key Considerations in Counterideological Work Against Terrorist Ideology," 532.

[462] Hassan, "Key Considerations in Counterideological Work Against Terrorist Ideology," 532.

[463] Hassan, "Key Considerations in Counterideological Work Against Terrorist Ideology," 532.

[464] Hassan, "Key Considerations in Counterideological Work Against Terrorist Ideology," 535.

[465] Hassan, "Key Considerations in Counterideological Work Against Terrorist Ideology," 535.

END NOTES

[466] Hassan, "Key Considerations in Counterideological Work Against Terrorist Ideology," 535.

[467] Jonathan Dean, "Coping With the Possibility of Terrorist Use of WMD." Report No. 15, (Stockholm, Sweden: The Weapons of Mass Destruction Commission, 2006).

[468] Dean, "Coping With the Possibility of Terrorist Use of WMD."

[469] Dean, "Coping With the Possibility of Terrorist Use of WMD," 8

[470] Dean, "Coping With the Possibility of Terrorist Use of WMD," 6

[471] Jessica Stern, "Mind Over Martyr: How to Deradicate Islamist Extremists," *Foreign Affairs,* vol. 89 (Tampa, FL: Council on Foreign Relations, January/Febraury, 2010), 95.

[472] Stern, "Mind Over Martyr: How to Deradicate Islamist Extremists," 95.

BIBLIOGRAPHY

CHAPTER 1

Alschuler, A. W. "Plea Bargaining and its History." *Law and Society Review*, vol. 13, no.2. New Jersey: John Wiley (1979): 211–243.

Alschuler, A. W. "Implementing the Criminal Defendant's Right to Trial: Alternatives to the Plea Bargaining System." *University of Chicago Law Review*, vol. 50, no. 3. Chicago: University of Chicago School of Law (1983): 931–1050.

Alschuler A. W. "Straining at Gnats and Swallowing Camels: The Selective Morality of Professor Bibas." *Cornell Law Review*, vol. 88, no. 5. New York: Cornell University School of Law (2003): 1412–1424.

Acevedo, R. "Is a Ban on Plea Bargaining an Ethical Abuse of Discretion? A Bronx County, New York Case Study." *Fordham Law Review*, vol. 64, no. 3. New York: Fordham University School of Law (1995): 987-1013.

Baldwin, J. and McConville, M. *Negotiated Justice: Pressures on Defendants to Plead Guilty*. London: Martin Robertson, 1977.

Baruch, C. "Through the Looking Glass: A Brief Comment on the Short Life and Unhappy Demise of the Singleton Rule." *Northern Kentucky Law Review*, vol. 27, no. 4. Kentucky: Northern Kentucky University (2000): 841-852.

Bergman, P. and Berman-Barrett, S. J. *The Criminal Law Handbook: Know your Rights, Survive the System.* 7th Ed., Nolo, Berkeley, California: Nolo, 2005.

Bibas, S. "Bringing Moral Values into Flawed Plea Bargaining System." *Cornell Law Review*, vol. 88, no. 5. New York: Cornell University School of Law (2003): 1425–1432.

Bibas, S. "Harmonizing Substantial Criminal Law Values and Criminal Procedure: The Case of Alford and Nolo Contendere Pleas." *Cornell Law Review*, vol. 88, no. 6. New York: Cornell University School of Law (2003): 1361–1411.

Bond, J. E. *Plea Bargaining and Guilty Pleas*. New York: Clark Boardman, 1975.

Callan, S. W. "An Experience in Justice Without Plea Negotiation." *Law and Society Review*, vol. 13, no. 2. New Jersey: John Wiley (1979): 327–347.

Cammack, M. E. and Garland, N. M. *Advanced Criminal Procedure*. St. Paul, MN: Thomson West, 2006.

Carlson, R. L. *Criminal Justice Procedure*, 5th Ed., Cincinnati, Ohio: Anderson Publishing Co, 1995.

Colquitt, J. A. "Ad Hoc Plea Bargaining." *Tulane Law Review*, vol.75, no.1. New Orleans: Tulane University Law School (2001): 695 - 775.

Dressler, J. *Understanding Criminal Procedure*. 2nd Ed., New York: Mathew Bender, 1997.

Easterbrook, F. H. "Plea Bargaining as Compromise. *Yale Law Journal,* vol. 101, no. 8. New Haven, CT: The Yale Law Company (1992): 1969 -1107.

Feeley, M. M. "Perspectives on Plea Bargaining." *Law and Society Review*, vol. 13, no. 2. New Jersey: John Wiley (1979): 199–209.

Fisher, G. *Plea Bargaining's Triumph: A History of Plea Bargaining in America*. Stanford, California: Stanford University Press, 2000.

Friedman, S. L. "Preplea Discovery: Guilty Pleas and the Likelihood of Conviction at Trial." *University of Pennsylvania Law Review*, vol. 119. Philadelphia:

University of Pennsylvania School of Law (1971): 527–535.

Friedman, L. M. "Plea Bargaining in Historical Perspective." *Law and Society Review*, vol. 13, no.2. New Jersey: John Wiley (1979): 247–259.

Guidorizzi, D. D. "Should we Really "Ban" Plea Bargaining?: The Core Concerns of Plea Bargaining Critics." *Emory Law Journal*, vol.47. (1998): 753–783.

Gazal-Ayal, O. "Partial Ban on Plea Bargains." *Cardozo Law Review*, vol. 27. No. 5. New York: Benjamin Cardozo School of Law (2006): 2295–2349.

Haller, M. H. "Plea Bargaining: The Nineteenth Century Context." *Law and Society Review*, vol. 13. New Jersey: John Wiley (1979): 272 - 279.

Herzog, S. "The Relationship between Public Perceptions of Crime Seriousness and Support for Plea Bargaining Practices in Israel: A factional Survey Approach." *Journal of Criminal Law and Criminology*, vol. 94. Chicago: Northwestern University School of Law (2003): 103-131.

Heumann, M. *Plea Bargaining: The Experiences of Prosecutors, Judges and Defense Attorneys.* Chicago: The University of Chicago Press, 1978.

Keane, P. Discussion with him on July 19, 2006. Golden Gate University School of Law, San Francisco, California, 2006.

Lafave, W. R., Israel, J. H. and King, N. J. *Criminal Procedure.* St. Paul. MN. Thomson West, 2004.

Langbein, J. H. "Torture and Plea Bargaining." *The University of Chicago Law Review*, vol. 46, no. 1. Chicago: University of Chicago (1978): 3–22.

Langbein, J. H. "Understanding the Short History of Plea Bargaining." *Law and Society Review*, vol. 13. New Jersey: John Wiley (1979): 161–271.

Langbein, J. H. "On the Myth of Written Constitutions: The Disappearance of Criminal Jury Trial." *Harvard Journal of Law and Public Policy*, vol.15, no.1. Cambridge, MA: Harvard University Press (1992): 119–127.

Lynch, T. "Rethinking the Petty Offense Doctrine." *The Kansas Journal of Law and Public Policy*, vol. 4. Kansas: University of Kansas School of Law (1994): 7-19.

Lynch, T. "The Case Against Plea Bargaining." *Regulation*, vol. 26. no. 3. Washington D.C: Cato Institute (2003): 28–31.

Mather, L. M. "Comments on the History of Plea Bargaining." *Law and Society Review*, vol.13. New Jersey: John Wiley (1979): 281–285.

Maynard, D. W. (1984). *Inside Plea Bargaining: The Language of Negotiation*. New York. Plenum Press.

McDonald, W. F. and Cramer, J. A. (eds.) *Plea Bargaining*. Lexington, Massachusetts: Lexington Books, 1980.

McDonald, W. F. *Plea Bargaining: Critical Issues and Common Practices* – Research Report, July 1985. Washington. D.C. United States Department of Justice, 1985.

Mnookin, J. L. "Uncertain Bargains: The Rise of Plea Bargaining in America." *Stanford Law Review*, vol. 57, no. 3. Stanford, CA: Stanford University (2005): 1721–1743.

Nardulli, P. F., Eisenstein, J., and Flemming, R. B. *The Tenor of Justice: Criminal Courts and the Guilty Plea Process*. Urbana: University of Illinois Press, 1988.

Palmer, J. "Abolishing Plea Bargaining: An End to the same old Song and Dance." *American Journal of Criminal Law*, vol. 26. Texas: University of Texas (1999): 505–536.

Robin, G. D. *Introduction to the Criminal Justice System*, 3rd Ed., New York, HarperCollins, 1987.

Rosett, A. and Cressey, D. R. *Justice by Consent: Plea Bargains in the American Courthouse*. Philadelphia: J. B. Lippincott Company, 1976.

Ross, J. E. "The Entrenched Position of Plea Bargaining in United States Legal Practice." *American Journal of Comparative Law*, vol. 54. Michigan: American Society of Comparative (2006): 717–732.

Sandefur, T. "In Defense of Plea Bargaining." *Regulation*, vol. 26. no. 3. Washington D.C: Cato Institute (2003): 28–31.

Schulhofer, S. J. "Is Plea Bargaining Inevitable?" *Harvard Law Review*, vol. 97. no. 5. Cambridge, MA: Harvard University Press (1984): 1037–1107.

Schulhofer, S. J. "Plea Bargaining as Disaster." *Yale Law Journal*, vol. 101. New Haven, CT: The Yale Law Journal Company (1992): 1979–1933.

Scott, R. E. and Stuntz, W. J. "Plea Bargaining as Contract." *101 Yale Law Journal*, vol. 101. New Haven, CT: The Yale Law Journal Company (1992): 1909–1968.

Scott, R. E. and Stuntz, W. J. "A Reply: Imperfect Bargains, Imperfect Trials and Innocent Defendants." *Yale Law Journal*, vol. 101. New Haven, CT: The Yale Law Journal Company (1992): 2011–2015.

Scharf, M. P. "Trading Justice for Efficiency: Plea Bargaining and International Tribunals." *Journal of International Criminal Justice*, vol. 2. Oxford: Oxford University Press (2004): 1070 –1081.

Smith, D. A. "The Plea Bargaining Controversy." *Journal of Criminal Law and Criminology*, vol. 77. Chicago: Northwestern University School of Law (1986): 949–967.

Stuntz, W. J. "Plea Bargaining and Criminal Law's Disappearing Shadow." *117 Harvard Law Review*, vol. 117. Cambridge, MA: Harvard University Press (2004): 2548–2569.

Vogel, M. E. "The Social Origins of Plea Bargaining: Conflict and the Law in the Process of State Formation 1830 – 1860." *Law and Society Review*, vol.33. no. 1. New Jersey: John Wiley (1999): 161–246.

Van Cleave, R. A. "An Offer you Can't Refuse? Punishment Without Trial in Italy and United States: The Search for Truth and an Efficient Criminal Justice System." *Emory International Law Review*, vol. 11. Atlanta: Emory University School of Law (1997): 419–469.

White, W. S. "A Proposal for Reform of the Plea Bargaining Process." *University of Pennsylvania Law Review*, vol. 119. Philadelphia: University of Pennsylvania School of Law (1971): 439–465.

Wininger, R. A. "The Abolition of Plea Bargaining: A Case Study of El Paso County, Texas." *University of California Los Angeles Law Review*, vol. 35. California: University of California Press (1987): 265–313.

CHAPTER 2

Archer, F. *Crime and the Psychic World.* New York: William Marrow and Company, 1969.

Bern, D. J., and Honorton, C. "Does Psi Exist? Replicable Evidence for an Anomalous Process of Information Transfer." *Psychological Bulletin,* vol. 115. Washington D.C: American Psychological Association (1994): 4-18.

Braude, S. E. *ESP and Psychokinesis: A Philosophical Examination.* Philadelphia: Temple University Press, 1979.

Broughton, R. *Parapsychology the Controversial Science.* New York: Ballantine, 1991.

Brink, F. "Parapsychology and Criminal Investigation." *International Criminal Police Review,* vol. 134. Lyon, France: Saint Cloud (1960): 3-8.

Carrington, H. *The Story of Psychic Science.* Whitefish, MT: Kessinger Publishing, 1997.

Cohen, D. *ESP: The Search Beyond the Senses.* New York: Harcourt, 1989.

Colman, A. M. (ed)., *Controversies in Psychology.* 2nd Ed., New York: Longman, 1995.

Cordon, L. A. *Popular Psychology: An Encyclopedia.* Westport, CT: Greenwood Press, 2005.

Gerberth, V. J. *Practical Homicide Investigations: Tactics, Procedures, and Forensic Techniques,* 4th Ed. Boca Raton: CRC Press, 2006.

Goode, E. *Paranormal Beliefs: A Sociological Introduction.* Illinois: Waveland Press, 2000.

Guarino, R. "The Police and Psychics," *Psychic,* (June 1975): 9-15.

Forer, B. R, "The Fallacy of Personal Validation: A Classroom Demonstration of Gullibility," *Journal of Abnormal and Social Psychology,* vol. 44, no. 1. Washington D.C: American Psychological Association (1949): 118-123.

Hibbard, W. S., Worring, R. W., and Brennan, R. S. *Psychic Criminology: A Guide for Using Psychics in Investigations.* Springfield: Charles C. Thomas Publisher, 2002.

Hicks, R. *The Psychic World of Law Enforcement.* New York: Warner, 1990.

Hines, T. *Psychic Crime Detection.* New York: Elsevier, 1992.

Jaegers, B. *Psychometry, The Science of Touch.* Sappington, MO: Arie Productions, 1980.

Jaegers, B. *The Psychic Paradigm.* New York: Berkley, 1988.

Kutz, P. "Is Parapsychology a Science?" *Skeptical Inquirer,* vol. 3. Amherst, NY: Committee for Skeptical Inquiry (1978): 14-32.

Lyons, A. and Truzzi, M. *The Blue Sense: Psychic Detectives and Crime.* New York: The Mysterious Press, 1991.

Martinez, L. "Looking into the Crystal Ball." *Law Enforcement Technology,* vol.31, no.7. Fort Atkinson, WI: Officer.com (2004): 52-59.

May, E. C. "The American Institutes for Research Review of the Department of Defense's STAR GATE Program: A Commentary." *Journal of Scientific Exploration,* vol.10, no. 1. Petaluma, CA: Society for Scientific Exploration (1996): 89-107.

May, M. "Police Consult Psychics." *The Daily Californian,* California: Berkeley, (April 20, 1990), 15.

Myers, N., and Czetli, S. N. *Silent Witness: The True Story of a Psychic Detective.* New York: St. Martins Press, 1995.

Nickell, J. (ed), *Psychic Sleuths: ESP and Sensational Cases.* New York: Prometheus Books, 1994.

Pogash, C. *Seduced by Madness: The True Story of the Susan Polk Murder Case.* New York: HarperCollins, 2008.

Randi, J. "Atlanta Child Murderer: Psychics' Failed Visions." *The Skeptical Inquirer,* Amherst, NY: Committee for Skeptical Inquiry (1982): 12-13.

Reiser, M., L. Ludwig, S. SAXE, and C. Wagner, "An Evaluation of the Use of Psychics in the Investigation of Major Crimes." *Journal of Police Science and Administration.* vol.7, no.1. International Association of Police Chiefs. (1979): 18-25.

Rhine, J. B. *Extra-Sensory Perception.* Boston: Boston Society for Psychic Research, 1935.

Rhine, J. B. "The Present Outlook on the Question of Psi in Animals." *Journal of Parapsychology,* vol.15. Columbus, OH: Parasychological Association (1951): 230-251.

Rhine, J. B. "A New Case of Experimenter Unreliability." *Journal of Parapsychology,* vol. 38. Columbus, OH: Parasychological Association (1974): 137-153.

Rhine, J. B. *Parapsychology Today.* New York: Citadel, 1988.

Roll, W. G., and Williams, B. J. "Quantum Theory, Neurobiology, and Parapsychology," In Krippner S., and Friedman, H. L., *Mysterious Minds: The Neurobiology of*

Psychics, Mediums, and Other Extraordinary People. Connecticut, Abc-Clio, 2010.

Stoeber, M., and Meynell, H. (Ed), *Critical Reflections on the Paranormal.* New York: State University of New York Press, 1996.

Wheeler, J. A. "Point of View: Drive the Pseudos Out." *Skeptical Inquirer,* vol.3. Amherst, NY: Committee for Skeptical Inquiry (1979): 12-13.

Willensky, D. *Criminal Minds.* New York: McGraw Hill, 1989.

Wilson, C. *Psychic Detectives.* San Francisco: Mercury House, 1985.

Wolman, B. *Handbook of Parapsychology.* New York: Van Nostrand, 1984.

CHAPTER 3

Azrael, D., Miller, M., and Hemmenway, D. "Are Household Firearms Stored Safely? It Depends on Whom You Ask." *Pediatrics,* vol. 106, no. 3. Illinois: American Academy of Pediatrics (2000): e31.

Baker, D. J. "Collective Criminalization and the Constitutional Right to Endanger Others." *Criminal Justice Ethics,* vol. 28, no. 2. New York: Routledge (2009): 168-200.

Cummings, P., Grossman, D.C., Rivara, F. P., Koepsell, T. D. "State Gun Safe Storage Laws and Child Mortality Due to Firearms." *Journal of the American Medical Association,* vol. 278. Chicago: American Medical Association (1997): 1084-1086.

Eisenberg, A. "Smart' Guns Can Check Identities Before Firing." *New York Times,* New York: New York Times (September 10, 1998): Section G, Page 3.

Frattaroli, S., Webster, D. W., and Teret, S. P. "Unintentional Gun Injuries, Firearm Design, and Prevention: What We Know, What We Need to Know, and What Can Be Done." *Journal of Urban Health: Bulletin of the New York Academy of Medicine,* vol. 79, no.1. New York: New York Academy of Medicine (2002): 49-59.

Glick, S. "Smart" Guns Dumb Idea, Won't End Firearm Abuse." *Houston Chronicle.* Houston, TX: Houston Chronicle (September 21, 1998): Section A.

Hemenway, D. "Regulation of Firearms." *The New England Journal of Medicine.* vol. 339. no. 12. Boston: NEJM Group (1998): 843-845.

Hemenway, D. *Private Guns, Public Health.* Ann Arbor: The University of Michigan Press, 2006.

Kopel, D. B. "Treating Guns like Consumer Products." *University of Pennsylvania Law Review,* vol.148. Philadelphia: University of Pennsylvania School of Law (2000): 1214-1224.

Leonardatos, C., Blackman, P. H., and Kopel, D. "Smart Guns/Foolish Legislators: Finding the Right Public Safety Laws, and Avoiding the Wrong Ones." *Connecticut Law Review,* vol.34. Hartford, CT: University of Connecticut School of Law (2001/2): 157-219.

Peterson, I. "Smart Guns" Setting Off Debate: How Smart Will They Really Be?" *New York Times.* New York: New York Times (October 22, 1998): A1, B7.

Rivara, F. P., and Kellerman, A. L. "Reducing the Misuse of Firearms," In LS Doll, SE Bonzo, and DA Sleet, (eds.), *Handbook of Injury and Violence Prevention.* New York: Springer (2007): 311-330.

Robinson K. D., Teret, S. P., Vernick, J. S., and Webster, D. W. "Personalized Guns: Reducing Gun Deaths Through Design Changes." Baltimore: John Hopkins Center for Gun Policy and Research (1996).

Sinauer, N., Annest, J., and Mercy, J. A. "Unintentional, Nonfatal Firearm-Related Injuries: A Preventable Public Health Burden." *Journal of the American Medical*

Association, Chicago: American Medical Association (1996): 1740-1743.

Smith, K. C. "Is this a Smart Gun?" *Handguns.* (January 2000): 54.

Sorenson, S.B., and Berk, R.A. "Young Guns: An Empirical Study of Persons who Use a Firearm in a Suicide or a Homicide." *Injury Prevention,* vol.5. London: British Medical Journal (1999): 280–283.

Sorenson, S. B. "Regulating Firearms as a Consumer Product." *Science.* vol. 286, no. 5444. Chicago: Association for the Advancement of Science (1999): 1481-1482.

Teret, S. P., and Wintemute, G. J. "Policies to Prevent Firearm Injuries." *Health Affairs.* vol. 12, no. 4. Bethesda, MD: Health Affairs (1993): 97-108.

Teret, S. P., and Baker, S. P. "Children Shooting Guns: A Failure in Product Design." *Injury Prevention.* vol.1, no.3. London: British Medical Journal (1995): 139.

Teret, S. P., DeFrancesco, S., Hargarten, S. W., and Robinson, K.D. "Making Guns Safer." *Issues in Science and Technology,* vol.14, no. 4. Texas: National Academy of Sciences (1998): 37-40.

Teret, S. P., Webster, D. W., Vernick, J. S., Smith, T. W., Leff, D., Wintemute, G. J., Cook, P. J., Hawkins, D. F., Kellermann, A. L., Sorenson, S. B., and DeFrancesco. "Support For New Policies To Regulate Firearms: Results of Two National Surveys." *The New England Journal of Medicine,* vol.339, no.12. Boston: NEJM Group (1998): 813-818.

Vernick, J. S., Meisel, Z. F., Teret, S. P., Milne, J. S., and Hargarten, S. W. "I didn't Know the Gun was Loaded": An Examination of Two Safety Devices that Can Reduce the Risk of Unintentional Firearm Injuries." *Journal of Public Health Policy,* vol.20. Hants: Palgrave Macmillan (1999): 427-440.

Vernick, J. S., and Teret, S. P. "Point/Counterpoint: A Public Health Approach to Regulating Firearms as

Consumer Products." *University of Pennsylvania Law Review*, vol.148. Philadelphia: University of Pennsylvania School of Law (2000): 1193-1211.

Violence Policy Center, "The False Hope of the Smart" Gun," www.vpc.org/fact-sht/smartgun.htm.

Violence Policy Center, "Iron River: Gun Violence and Illegal Firearms Trafficking on the U.S.-Mexico Border," Washington, D.C. (April 2009).

Wayne, L. "Smart Guns Proving to Be No Quick Fix for Firearm Violence." *New York Times.* New York: New York Times (1999): A24.

Weiss, D. R. "Sandia National Laboratories, Smart Gun Technology Project: Final Report." Albuquerque, NM: Sandia National Laboratories, 1996.

Wintemute, G. J. "The Relationship Between Firearm Design and Firearm Violence: Handguns in the 1990s." *Journal of the American Medical Association,* vol.275, no.22. Chicago: American Medical Association (1996): 1749-1753.

Wintemute, G. J. "The Future of Firearm Violence: Building on Success." *Journal of the American Medical Association,* vol.281, no.5. Chicago: American Medical Association (1999): 475-478.

CHAPTER 4

Adogame, A. "The 419 Code as Business Unusual.Youth and the Unfolding of the Advance Fee Fraud Online Discourse." *Asian Journal of Social Sciences,* vol.37, no. 4. Leiden, The Netherlands: Brill (2009): 551-573.

Adomi, E. E., and Ugun, S. E. "Combating Cyber Crime in Nigeria." *The Electronic Library,* vol.26, no.5. Bingley, UK: Emerald Insights Group Publishing (2008): 716-725.

Axelrod, E. M. *Violence Goes to the Internet: Avoiding the Snare of the Net.* Springfield: Charles C Thomas Publishers, 2009.

Broadhurst, R. "Developments in the Global Law Enforcement of Cyber-Crime." *Policing: An International Journal of Police Strategies and Management,* vol.29, no.3. Bingley, UK: Emerald Insights Group Publishing (2006): 408-432.

Dixon, R. "Nigerian Cyber Scammers." *Los Angeles Times.* Los Angeles, October 20, 2005.

Edelson, E. *Scamorama.* New York: The Disinformation Company, 2006.

Goldsmith, J. and Wu, T. *Who Controls the Internet? Illusions of a Borderless World.* Oxford: Oxford University Press, 2006.

Kao, D., and Wang, S. "The IP Address and Time in Cyber-Crime Investigation." *Policing: An International Journal of Police Strategies and Management,* vol.32, no.2. Bingley, UK: Emerald Insights Group Publishing (2009).

Oriola, T. A. "Advance Fee Fraud on the Internet. Nigeria's Regulatory Response." *Computer Law and Security Review,* vol. 21, Oxford: Elsevier (2005): 237-248.

Smith, R. G., Holmes, M. N., and Kaufman, P. "Nigerian Advance Fee Fraud." *Trends in Crime and Criminal Justice,* vol.121. Canberra, Australia: Australian Institute of Criminology (1999): 1-12.

Stajano, F., and Wilson, P. "Understanding Scam Victims. Seven Principles for Systems Security." *Technical Report,* no.754. Cambridge: Cambridge University, August, 2009.

Stevens, A. *"419": The Story of Advance Fee Fraud.* Baltimore: PublishAmerica, 2006.

Tive, C. *419 Scam: Exploits of the Nigerian Con Man.* Bloomington, IN: iUniverse, 2006.

Zuckoff, M. "How a Massachusetts Psychotherapist Fell for a Nigerian E-mail Scam." *The New Yorker.* New York: Conde Nast, May 15, 2006.

CHAPTER 5

Atran, S. "Genesis of Suicide Terrorism." *Science*, vol.299, no.5612. Washington D.C: American Association for the Advancement of Science (2005): 1534-1539.

Bjorgo, T., (eds.), *Root Causes of Terrorism: Myths, Reality and Ways Forward.* Oxford: Routledge, 2005.

Brooks, S. G. *Producing Security: Multinational Corporations, Globalization and the Changing Calculus of Conflict.* Princeton: Princeton University Press, 2005.

Cerny, P. G. "Terrorism and the New Security Dilemma." *Naval War College Review*, vol.58, no.1. Newport, RI: Naval War College (2005): 11-33.

Collins, R. "Suicide Bombers: Warriors of the Middle Class." *Foreign Policy.* Washington D.C: Foreign Policy Group, 2008.

Crenshaw, M. "Terrorism, Strategies and Grand Strategies," In Cronin, A. K., and Ludes, J. M., *Attacking Terrorism: Elements of a Grand Strategy.* Washington D.C: Georgetown University Press, 2004.

Cronin, A. K. "Rethinking Sovereignty: American Strategy in the Age of Terror." *Survival: Global Politics & Strategy*, vol.44, no. 2. Washington D.C: International Institute for Strategic Studies (2002): 119-139.

Cronin, A. K. "Behind the Curve: Globalization and International Terrorism." *International Security*, vol.27, no.3. Cambridge, MA: Kennedy School of Government, Harvard University (2002/3): 30-58.

Cronin, A. K. and Ludes, J. M. *Attacking Terrorism: Elements of a Grand Strategy.* Washington D.C: Georgetown University Press, 2004.

Dandurand, Y. and Chin, A. "Links Between Terrorism and Other Forms of Crime." International Centre for Criminal Law Reform. British Columbia, Canada: International Centre for Criminal Law Reform, 2004.

Forst, B. *Terrorism, Crime, and Public Policy, Cambridge.* Cambridge: University Press, 2009.

Friedman, T. L. *The Lexus and the Olive Tree.* New York: Anchor Books, 2006.

Gilligan, J. *Violence: Reflections on Our Deadliest Epidemic.* London: Jessica Kingsley, 2000.

Groebel, J., and Goldstein, J. H. *Terrorism: Psychological Perspectives.* Sevilla: Universida De Sevilla, 1989.

Gulke, A., (1995). *The Age of Terrorism and the International Political System*, London, I.B. Tauris.

Gulke, A. *Terrorism and Global Disorder: Political Violence in the Contemporary World.* London: I.B. Tauris, 2006.

Hoge, J., and Rose, G. Terrorism and the New War, New York: Public Affairs, 2001.

Horgan, J. *The Psychology of Terrorism.* London: Routledge, 2005.

Horgan, J. "From Profiles to Pathways and Roots to Routs: Perspectives from Psychology on Radicalization into Terrorism." *The Annals of the American Academy of Political and Social Science,* vol.618, no.1. Thousand Oaks, CA: Sage Publications (2008) 80-94.

Hudson, R. A. "The Sociology and Psychology of Terrorism: Who becomes a Terrorist and Why?" Washington D.C: Library of Congress, 1999.

Jantzen, R. H. "Dynamics of New York City Crime." Paper presented at the *66th International Atlantic Economic Conference.* Montreal, Canada: October 2008.

Johnson, T. A. *The War on Terrorism: A Collision of Values, Strategies, and Societies.* Boca Raton: CRC Press, 2008.

Kaldor, M. *New and Old Wars: Organized Violence in a Globalized Era.* Stanford, CA: Stanford University Press, 2001.

Kegley Jr., C. W., (eds), *International Terrorism: Characteristics, Causes, Controls.* New York: St. Martin's Press, 1990.

Kirshner, J. "Globalization, American Power, and International Security." *Political Science Quarterly,* vol.123, no.3. New York: Academy of Political Science (2008): 363-389.

Kirshner, J. (eds.), *Globalization and National Security.* New York: Routledge, 2006.

Krueger, A. B., and Maleckova, J. "The Economics and the Education of Suicide Bombers: Does Poverty Cause Terrorism?" *The New Republic.* Washington D.C: The New Republic, June 24, 2002.

Laqueur, W. "Left, Right and Beyond: The Changing Face of Terror," In Hoge, J., and Rose, G., (eds.), *Terrorism and the New War.* New York: Public Affairs, 2001.

Lawrence, H. (eds.), *Terrorism: Roots, Impact, Responses.* Westport, CT: Praeger, 1992.

Lombroso, C. *The Criminal Man.* Turin: Fratella Bocca, 1876.

Lynch, M. "Globalization and Arab Security" In Jonathan Kirshner (ed.) *Globalization and National Security.* New York: Routledge, 2006.

Mousseau, M. "Market Civilization and its Clash with Terror." *International Security*, vol.27, no3. Cambridge, MA: Kennedy School of Government, Harvard University (2002/3): 5-29.

Nassar, J. R. *Globalization and Terrorism: The Migration of Dreams and Nightmares.* Lanham, MD: Rowman & Littlefield, 2005.

Plaw, A. *Targeting Terrorists: A License to Kill?* Aldershot, Ashgate, (2008).

Post, J. M., "The Psychological Dynamics of Terrorism," In Richardson, L., (eds.), *The Roots of Terrorism.* New York: Routledge, 2006.

Rapport, D. C. "The Fourth Wave: September 11 in the History of Terrorism." *Current History: A Journal of Contemporary World Affairs,* vol.100, no.650. Philadelphia: Current History (2001): 419-424.

Richardson, L. (eds.), *The Roots of Terrorism.* New York: Routledge, 2006.

Silke, A. (eds.), *Terrorists, Victims and Society: Psychological Perspectives on Terrorism and its Consequences.* Chichester: John Wiley, 2003.

Stern, J. "Mind Over Martyr: How to Deradicate Islamist Extremists." *Foreign Affairs.* Tampa, FL: Council on Foreign Relations (2010): 89-95.

Stiglitz, J. E. *Globalization and its Discontents.* New York: W.W. Norton, 2002.

Whittaker, D. J. *Terrorists and Terrorism in Contemporary World.* London: Routledge, 2004.

INDEX

ABOUT THE AUTHOR

NORBERT EBISIKE, SJD. , is a criminologist and legal scholar. Dr. Ebisike is a graduate of the University of Pennsylvania, Golden Gate University, the University of Kent, Canterbury, and the University of Westminster, London. His publications include *Offender Profiling in the Courtroom: The Use and Abuse of Expert Witness Testimony,* Praeger (2008); *An Appraisal of Forensic Science Evidence in Criminal Proceedings,* Greenway Press (2001); *The Investigative and Evidential Uses of Cheiloscopy (Lip Prints),* Criminal Law Bulletin (2011); and *The Evidence of Children,* Criminal Law Bulletin (2008). His current research interests include forensic science evidence, neurocriminology, children and the law, offender profiling, terrorism, and socio-legal studies.

Made in the USA
Monee, IL
04 November 2026

67381849R10115